"*Exposing Emot[ional Manipulation] is [a powerful] and timely book t[hat addresses the decep]tive tactics of emotional manipulation and control. Ryan LeStrange delivers profound biblical insights and practical strategies that empower individuals to recognize and break free from the grip of manipulation, intimidation, and guilt. With clarity and wisdom, he exposes the dark spiritual roots of these behaviors, offering a pathway to freedom and healing through the power of the Holy Spirit. This book is a must-read for anyone seeking to live in the liberty that Christ offers and to walk in healthy, godly relationships. It equips readers with the discernment needed to identify manipulative behaviors and the tools to overcome them, allowing the Holy Spirit to lead and guide them in truth and love."

—Apostle John Eckhardt, bestselling author,
Prayers That Route Demons

"Apostle Ryan LeStrange is one of my favorite preachers. The way he delivers his messages with revelation, passion, and zeal is powerful. His teachings are always spot-on and relatable. I have admired his teachings for years as he has unlocked powerful revelations on overcoming spiritual attacks, breaking curses, Jezebel, and learning to defeat demonic spirits that attempt to steal your destiny. I'm confident this book on dealing with emotional witchcraft is going to be a game changer. This book is necessary, and will help a multitude of leaders and believers get free. *Exposing Emotional Manipulation*, with its insight on this demonic stronghold, is going to be a blessing for many. Apostle Ryan isn't just giving us insight on something he read or learned from others; he is giving us insight on what he lived and overcame, which makes for an amazing read. I highly recommend this book."

—Sophia Ruffin-Wilson, founder, Sophia Ruffin Global; author, *It Will Be God*

"In *Exposing Emotional Manipulation*, Ryan LeStrange uncovers the subtle yet destructive forces that manipulate and control through emotions, offering a much-needed light on an often-overlooked form of spiritual warfare. With profound insight, Ryan exposes the tactics of the enemy, revealing how emotional manipulation can entangle even the most discerning believers. He writes, 'Emotional witchcraft is using controlling powers and techniques to override the will of another by manipulating his or her emotions,' offering readers both understanding and tools to break free. This book is a must-read for anyone seeking to protect their spiritual health and walk in the freedom that Christ offers."

Vladimir Savchuk, senior pastor, HungryGen Church;
author and speaker

"Apostle Ryan LeStrange's latest book offers a thought-provoking exploration of spiritual influence and manipulation. Drawing on biblical teachings and personal experiences, LeStrange examines the nature of godly guidance versus manipulative control. If you're seeking perspective on Christian leadership dynamics and spiritual discernment and want to know how to break free, this book is for you!"

Mike Signorelli, lead pastor, V1 Church; author,
Inherit Your Freedom and *Fire Starters*

"Ryan LeStrange's *Exposing Emotional Manipulation* is a powerful and timely guide for anyone seeking freedom from the insidious grip of manipulation and control. Grounded in biblical truth and offering practical, actionable strategies, this book exposes the spiritual dynamics behind emotional manipulation and provides a clear path to deliverance. LeStrange's wisdom and insight will empower readers to break free from the influence of wrong spirits and embrace the leading of the Holy Spirit, who guides us with love, not control. It is a must-read for those ready to reclaim their emotional and spiritual freedom."

Dr. Joel Tudman, senior pastor, The Faith Center

EXPOSING EMOTIONAL MANIPULATION

EXPOSING EMOTIONAL MANIPULATION

Break the Control,
Grow Relationally,
Heal Emotionally

RYAN LeSTRANGE

Chosen

a division of Baker Publishing Group
Minneapolis, Minnesota

© 2025 by Ryan LeStrange

Published by Chosen Books
Minneapolis, Minnesota
ChosenBooks.com

Chosen Books is a division of
Baker Publishing Group, Grand Rapids, Michigan

Printed in the United States of America

All rights reserved. No part of this publication may be reproduced, stored in a retrieval system, or transmitted in any form or by any means—for example, electronic, photocopy, recording—without the prior written permission of the publisher. The only exception is brief quotations in printed reviews.

Library of Congress Cataloging-in-Publication Data
Names: LeStrange, Ryan, author.
Title: Exposing emotional manipulation : break the control, grow relationally, heal emotionally / Ryan LeStrange.
Description: Minneapolis, Minnesota : Chosen, a division of Baker Publishing Group, [2025] | Includes bibliographical references.
Identifiers: LCCN 2024059508 | ISBN 9780800773304 (paperback) | ISBN 9780800773342 (casebound) | ISBN 9781493452262 (ebook)
Subjects: LCSH: Control (Psychology)—Religious aspects—Christianity. | Manipulative behavior. | Interpersonal relations—Religious aspects—Christianity.
Classification: LCC BV4597.53.C62 L477 2025 | DDC 155—dc23/eng/20250425
LC record available at https://lccn.loc.gov/2024059508

Unless otherwise indicated, Scripture taken from the New King James Version®. Copyright © 1982 by Thomas Nelson. Used by permission. All rights reserved.

Scripture identified AMPC taken from the Amplified® Bible, Copyright © 1954, 1958, 1962, 1964, 1965, 1987 by The Lockman Foundation. Used by permission. lockman.org

Scripture quotations identified KJV are from the King James Version of the Bible.

Scripture quotations identified MSG are taken from *The Message*, copyright © 1993, 2002, 2018 by Eugene H. Peterson. Used by permission of NavPress. All rights reserved. Represented by Tyndale House Publishers.

Scripture quotations identified NASB taken from the (NASB®) New American Standard Bible®, Copyright © 1960, 1971, 1977, 1995, 2020 by The Lockman Foundation. Used by permission. All rights reserved. www.lockman.org

Cover design by Darren Welch Design

Baker Publishing Group publications use paper produced from sustainable forestry practices and postconsumer waste whenever possible.

25 26 27 28 29 30 31   7 6 5 4 3 2 1

I dedicate this book to those who have gone before me: generals, leaders, teachers, prophets, and proclaimers of God's Word. In a generation that often forgets our origins, I stand up to say, "I remember!" Thank you, trailblazers. Thank you, pioneers. Thank you, generals. You were necessary, and we will do our best to keep blazing the trail.

Contents

Foreword by Jenny Weaver 13

1. Emotional Witchcraft? 15
2. The Nice Church Lady 32
3. The Purpose of Godly Relationships 48
4. Manipulation Strategies Exposed 65
5. Types of Manipulators 82
6. Closing Open Doorways 99
7. Breaking Soul Ties and Evil Alliances 116
8. Growing Relationally 133
9. Healing Emotionally 150
10. Decrees and Prayers 166

Acknowledgments 185
Notes 187

Foreword

I remember meeting Ryan in April 2018. During this time, I was a worship leader who had just begun a traveling ministry, branched from a God-idea called "singing the Scriptures." I was introduced to Ryan's ministry via social media, saw him preaching, and started following his page. From there I was blessed to dive into his teachings and trainings, since I was coming from a small-town church where there was no prophetic or apostolic ministry. It was, to say the least, refreshing to connect with him.

The Lord called me from singing the Scriptures into teaching online; that developed into the Core Group, now an online and in-person mentorship ministry to more than twenty thousand people.

I'm no stranger to the topic of Ryan's book! I was a practicing Wiccan as a teenager and young adult, set free and delivered for many years. I now help people find deliverance and freedom from the lifestyle of witchcraft and the occult world.

This book does an excellent job of going beyond the idea that witchcraft comes from a person with a black pointy hat and cauldron who flies around on a broomstick. It explores things many don't delve into and breaks down the understanding of witchcraft in the realm of emotions and manipulation.

Being pulled into emotional manipulation can be a tool of witchcraft, sometimes learned from an overbearing, controlling parent; it's a demonic tool young children learn in a home where adults use emotional manipulation to try to control situations as they wish.

When such manipulation manifests in the life of an adult, it can be a vicious cycle. The person may know it only as their "normal," but it is far from normal in the kingdom of God! The Bible calls the works of the flesh "witchcraft" (Galatians 5:20). Ryan gives us tools we can use to recognize the ways people can be pulled into this through things like soul ties and other previously unrecognized types of manipulation.

I love to read a book when it feels like the book is "reading" me and my life, in a way! The Holy Ghost uses those "aha" moments through the words on the page to go deep into the soul to reveal truth and set us free. As you read this book, you will begin to experience the freedom that comes from the truth of the gospel. You will learn about godly relationships, life structure, order, and how to navigate your new seasons without using the old tactics.

Whether you struggle with emotional manipulation yourself, want to gain knowledge to help others, or know a person who is a victim or a manipulator, this book will help you navigate. It will give you language, ways to overcome, and ultimately, breakthrough. And I bless you in your new season of breakthrough in Jesus' name.

Jenny Weaver, Core Group

CHAPTER ONE

Emotional Witchcraft?

We have all faced moments in our lives in which we realized that our will was bent to the will of another in a way that was either frustrating or deeply troubling. Perhaps a close friend talked you into doing something outside of your normal boundaries, and you later sank into a pit of regret. Maybe it was a family member who pulled deeply on your heartstrings to get you to yield to their wishes, despite feeling clearly that God's Spirit in you was making objections. If you have been involved in the church for any length of time, you may have encountered a cunning leader who played on your deepest fears or greatest hopes to coerce you into doing something you didn't really want to do. Now, let me be clear: I'm not talking about doing things that stretch you or make you uncomfortable. Sometimes in our walk with God, we are stretched in a very healthy way! I'm talking about times when God's Spirit in you is throwing red flags and you're tempted to ignore them because people in your life compel you to bypass your convictions and attempt to dominate your will.

The enemy is cunning; he knows how to use every part of your life to try to bring deception and bondage. One of the most heinous things he does is operate through undercover domination. I call this "emotional witchcraft." That sounds severe!

You may ask, "What is emotional witchcraft?" Emotional witchcraft is using controlling powers and techniques to override the will of another by manipulating his or her emotions. Now we may know about easily identified forms of witchcraft, such as incantations or sorcery, fueled by demonic powers. But the root of *every* evil spiritual practice of witchcraft is rebellion. "For rebellion is as the sin of witchcraft, and stubbornness is as iniquity and idolatry. Because you have rejected the word of the LORD, he also has rejected you from being king" (1 Samuel 15:23).

Although this verse deals with God's repudiation of Saul as king, it also reveals the primary underlying principle for all dark spiritual practices—rebellion. Rebellion strikes and leads a person to worship and exalt the creation, not the Creator. This establishes a platform for demonic operations.

Another, lesser-known dimension of witchcraft is rooted in the flesh (also known as self-will, human nature, the "old man"). To uncover this, we need to look to the teachings of Paul in Galatians.

> Now the works of the flesh are manifest, which are these; Adultery, fornication, uncleanness, lasciviousness, idolatry, *witchcraft*, hatred, variance, emulations, wrath, strife, seditions, heresies, envyings, murders, drunkenness, revellings,

and such like: of the which I tell you before, as I have also told you in time past, that they which do such things shall not inherit the kingdom of God.

Galatians 5:19–21 KJV, emphasis added

As Paul lists the works of the flesh, he exposes the evil nature of carnality (that is, "doing things my way, for my satisfaction"). Notice that right there in the middle of this list, he places witchcraft!

Emotional manipulation as a form of witchcraft is a desire to control and bend the will of another person to "my way." It seeks to control those with unrenewed minds who are still living carnal or sensual lives. Men and women who learn how to dominate others can often get them to accommodate their will. These practices often begin at a young age. Children learn how to manipulate the emotions of parents, caregivers, teachers, and friends, trying to get them to do what they want them to do. As life brings painful experiences, people may cling to "feeling safe," which can then empower in them a controlling and dominating spirit.

Seeking to influence the will of another by acting on their emotions with your agenda in mind disregards their personhood, desires, boundaries, and health—that is evil work. Yet many people fall into this and use intimidation, play on guilt, or manipulate others in other ways into ungodly domination. This is satanic in nature!

The Holy Spirit was provided to lead us. He does not control, dominate, or oppress us. Instead, He provides much-needed insight, comfort, illumination, and guidance. He comes to strengthen us and assist us in our journey with God the Father.

But the Comforter (Counselor, Helper, Intercessor, Advocate, Strengthener, Standby), the Holy Spirit, Whom the Father will send in My name [in My place, to represent Me and act on My behalf], He will teach you all things. And He will cause you to recall (will remind you of, bring to your remembrance) everything I have told you.

John 14:26 AMPC

Demons bombard, push, and drive people. They work to overwhelm humans with temptation and pressure to get them to succumb to demonic desires and plans. In the same fashion, emotional manipulation seeks to overcome the will of an individual to achieve the desire of the person operating in manipulation This fleshly operation can easily become a demonic maneuver.

Areas of Vulnerability

A primary tool of emotional manipulation or witchcraft is playing on another person's feelings of guilt. Manipulative leaders learn how to see and to seize the vulnerabilities in others. They often create feelings of guilt in others who don't cooperate with their own dysfunction. I once dealt with a prophetic leader who operated in a heavy level of Jezebelic witchcraft. The Jezebel spirit is a dominating spirit that seeks out weak leaders and people it can control. In leaders, it can manifest as an unhealthy controlling spirit that disguises its heinous operations in spiritual language, but the fruit and motive are rotten! This leader surrounded himself with people who were looking for acceptance. His inner circle could see that behind the scenes, he was living a double life. He presented himself as a purity person publicly, but cussed and manifested extreme rage and dark manipulation in private. Those who witnessed these behaviors knew something was wrong, but they felt conflicted. They didn't want to disconnect, because the prophetic leader was known to curse those who did not obey him! He heavily used emotional manipulation and witchcraft, making people feel guilty if they left or withdrew; he would then attack and accuse them viciously.

This is a significant warning sign! When people demonize you for a simple disagreement or for independent thinking, pay attention! It can be a symptom of something much more profound. But please don't hear what I am *not* saying! I believe in bold leadership, godly accountability, and correction, but love must be the motivator. We are put on earth to serve the Lord and His people, not to bully and dominate them. Godly leaders point people to Christ, not themselves. They have a vision and a mandate that they are passionate about, but they submit it to Christ Jesus. As Paul wrote, "Imitate me, just as I also imitate Christ" (1 Corinthians 11:1). Christian leadership goes rogue when we forget our "why"!

Paul aimed to please God by leading people to Him. He understood that kingdom life and ministry are about revealing the King. He wasn't trying to build a fan club, but an activated family of believers who were beholding the King in all His glory. It was Jesus who ransomed us, called us, and redeemed us. All our work is rubbish if it does not please the King! This is the measuring line.

God will often come to challenge our hearts and purify our motives. This is a much-needed process for God's people, because it is easy to become puffed up and arrogant. We must never graduate from serving under and submitting to Christ. When we are truly walking with the Lord, we want to see God's best for other people. That may mean saying the hard things, rebuking, or correcting, but the spirit behind it is right! We are not to move in our strength or desire. We are to move *with* God and seek to please Him above all others. The enemy is skillful and knows how to come in with a sneak attack. Many times, we become vulnerable to emotional manipulation and associated witchcraft because of past painful experiences.

I knew a preacher who had grown up in a deeply troubled family and was later radically saved. All she really wanted to do was please God. Her passion for God the Father came from a deep desire to be loved and truly accepted. At times, that would lead her to radical acts of obedience; at other times, it would be a gateway through which demonic pressure could enter. In her early ministry, she pioneered a Bible study, and an older man who was a father-type figure came to support her fledgling work. She was excited to have his support and appreciated his wisdom and love. He spoke as a seasoned elder and confirmed the need for her Bible study in the region. She had a fractured and distant relationship with her biological father. Though she had prayed many prayers of healing, she continued to struggle with an inner desire to be loved and accepted. The presence of this father-type figure spoke to that wound. She had always had keen spiritual insight and was known for her prophetic gift; it was one of the things that drew people to her Bible studies. They loved her ability to bring the Word of God to life passionately, while ministering with prophetic boldness. People would receive accurate prophetic words and life-changing ministry during her gatherings.

But this father-figure man had a history of going from ministry to ministry and finding fault in them. As he told his version of events, he always gave valid and deeply spiritual reasons, yet on prayerful examination, the evidence was clear: He had leadership issues. His description of his journey was veiled in language that made you feel guilty if you questioned his rationale. In many ways, it was an ominous sign. But the young prophetic leader overlooked it! Why didn't she see it? I believe that due to her past pain and her unhealed desire to be loved and accepted, this man's "support" and words moved her to pass up her God-given discernment!

Pause and think about that. Have you ever found yourself in that place? You knew there was a red flag, but you allowed the words of another to bypass that check you felt in your spirit. You accepted something you would have normally rejected. I know that I have made that mistake too many times!

In the end, the relationship between the young prophet and the older man devolved as he used condemnation tactics to back her into a corner. Finally, her eyes were opened. She saw that his actions were manipulating her and causing confusion in her team. He had pulled on her emotions to bring her into a place of deception.

What can we learn from this story? First, the importance of personal deliverance and healing. We need to take time to allow the Lord's healing power to wash over our minds and heal our hearts. We also need a deep relationship with the Holy Spirit, asking Him to reveal areas of vulnerability and weakness, so that we are watchful of ourselves and don't fall prey to the tactics of the enemy.

Protecting Your "Big Why"

"Beloved, I pray that you may prosper in all things and be in health, just as your soul prospers" (3 John 1:2). Coming into alignment with your purpose is majestically beautiful! When we find the God-ordained rhythm of our lives and fully embrace it, there is an unmatched level of synchronicity. I believe this verse speaks about the emotional, spiritual, and economic prosperity that flow when we discover and embrace our "big why."

Your "big why" is the reason why you were chosen to be alive on earth, in this time! What is the reason that God reserved you for this season? The prophetic anointing helps unveil our why! God gives us glimpses of our future. I describe it as God cracking open the door and taking you into the possibility of what could be when you align with heaven's purpose for your life. Each of us is on an unfolding journey of discovery! Think of it: We open God's Word and suddenly, something jumps off the page at us. Then we pray, and bam! We see or hear something that brings us further insight. Next, God sends someone who shares a prophetic word with us and it further confirms and fuels our sense of God's heart toward us.

Prayer is a journey of discovery. The more we seek the Father, the more we begin to understand the vast nature of His love. He unfolds mysteries and revelations to us as His sons and daughters. As we pray, we glimpse God's heart. This brings us a deeper awareness of who He is and who we are called to be in Him! In this journey, God brings us to discover His will through other prophetic moments. As these things come together, we're led into true alignment with God's plan for us.

What does that look like? It is the full realization and pursuit of God's intended purpose, the embrace of God's original intent before you were transgressed by sin. It is returning to the original plan and purpose for your life. It unlocks a level of prosperity, because the soul begins to flourish. Your mind, will, and emotions come into agreement with God and your born-again spirit to fully embrace your destiny. A new level of joy is unlocked as you step into your authentic self and true plan. When you discover your purpose and unite it with your passion, it becomes something beyond "work"—you discover your life's work.

Living with purpose means answering the critical question, What is my contribution? What is the purpose for which I was born? God has woven your abilities, gifts, favor, and personality together as He has in order to connect with your divine purpose.

It is imperative to understand that the gift of God in your life will open the right doors for you. Recently, I have been saying to myself, *If it's for me, it will find me!* In other words, I am not kicking down any door; I am not chasing something that does not open to me. I am boldly resting in faith that if God has ordained it for me, then it will find me.

"A man's gift makes room for him and brings him before great men" (Proverbs 18:16). Your gift is something you do with ease that others struggle with. You see how others struggle and wonder why it is difficult for them. Each of us has unique gifts that connect with our "big why." Your gift becomes a breakthrough and blessing for others. The teacher answers the deep questions people have been pondering. The prophet peels back the layers and reveals the mysteries of the will of God. The minister of helps comes into a ministry and quickly starts plugging holes through service that releases the ministry gift to pray, study, and move up to a higher level of function. In each of these examples, the divine purpose also shifts the lives of those around them.

Your gift is powerful! The enemy wants to keep you operating far below the place in which God has prepared for you to live. If he can get you out of your purpose, he can trap you in frustration, because operating in your purpose unlocks joy. It is that divine rhythm in your life. It is the alignment of eternity and the now. It is the space where perspective shifts and things make sense; you see why you went through the fights you went through. Your purpose is powerful! It will get you up early and keep you awake late at night. It is the engine of passion in your life. When you tap into your purpose, you unlock your passion. No purpose is identical, and no purpose is unimportant. Let me say it this way; there are no big *I*'s and little *you*'s in the kingdom of God! His call upon your life is important to the world around you, which is why hell has fought against you so aggressively.

> For we are God's [own] handiwork (His workmanship), recreated in Christ Jesus, [born anew] that we may do those good works which God predestined (planned beforehand) for us [taking paths which He prepared ahead of time], that we should walk in them [living the good life which He prearranged and made ready for us to live].
>
> Ephesians 2:10 AMPC

Our purpose begins with the understanding that we were handcrafted by the Almighty for His divine design. Nothing was by accident. He skillfully created our personality to match our purpose. When we realize this, we stop trying to change everything about ourselves and begin to partner with God's true intention for our lives.

Of course, the enemy doesn't want to let this go on; he tries his best to distract and delay us. He realizes that we are a threat when we fully embrace God's plan for us. The embrace only happens when we are led by God's Spirit to discover His heart for us. This is one reason why emotional manipulation becomes so dangerous! It leads us to the desires and designs of another person, instead of designs God intended for us. This dilutes our sense of purpose and creates unnecessary delays and distractions, while increasing our frustration. Listening to God's "yes" and His "no" is vital for you!

Enticements and Seductions

Another tool of witchcraft (and another aspect of manipulation) is enticement. The enemy will try to lure you off course by offering you things. This appeal to lust ("I want it now!") can play on your heartstrings and cause you to align with dangerous people and places. I remember a vivid example in my own life of spiritual and emotional seduction. For many years in my younger days, I carried a burden and passion for media. I had gone on a long journey of surrendering that desire to the Lord, as I was in a time of radical obedience and personal reformation. The Lord had me on an intense journey of deliverance and spiritual growth. Suddenly, an opportunity arose to create a Christian television show targeted at young people. I was in my early twenties and sincerely prayed over this opportunity. I felt the Lord's "yes" on the project and embarked on a remarkable journey.

My team and I traveled to interview well-known figures in Christian youth culture. We talked to young people about their hopes and challenges. We filmed a teaching segment and edited it all together creatively, and we were excited about the opportunity to do something unique in this space. We completed the edit of our pilot episode and presented it to the network. We were filled with anticipation as we awaited their answer. Then came the news that we had been waiting for after this long and arduous work: The network greenlighted our project! It was a "go." To say I was excited is a vast understatement! Then, the unthinkable happened. The entire network was sold—and as quickly as the opportunity had come, it disappeared. So many questions swirled in my mind, but I was determined to trust God even though I didn't understand it.

This is one of the big mysteries of our walk with the Lord—the time of the unknown. The space in which things don't work the way *we* thought they would. They may be called "the valley experiences," where the pain and the betrayal are intense. Sometimes, we eagerly search for a logical answer, but we come up empty. We can either give our "why?" to the Lord or allow it to create a place of bitterness in our hearts. I found my solace in the realization that God was and is sovereign. I gave my many months of work and my disappointment to the Lord, and I moved on.

Now, let me say this: Both God and the devil know our wildest dreams and most significant hopes! When the enemy sends someone into your life with a manipulative demon, they often work to entice you. They do so by speaking to the part of your soul that holds unmet expectations and desires. I experienced this exact thing during that particular season.

For context, let me give a little backstory. I was saved in my late teens and then led to move across the country to go to Bible college. The things of God were new to me, as I was not raised in church. I fought a lot of darkness. Jesus had radically saved and delivered me, and I became determined to serve Him and do my best to stay linked up with His plan for my life. He sent me to the ministry of a mighty man of God and told me to stay put. That is where I was as our television project came screeching to a halt. During this time, the enemy tried a masterful distraction tactic on me. A very successful minister asked to meet with me. As soon as I met with him, he began to tell me about all his television connections. He then told me that he would love to introduce me to people in the Christian television world. These were leaders of networks, people who could get that now-shelved show revived.

I still remember that conversation. My bruised soul was reeling from the apparent failure of my project, and suddenly this person was dangling a carrot of opportunity in front of me. As I sat there, it all sounded so good to my mind. The minister spoke skillfully to my desire and to what I believed was a God-ordained dream, but I felt something else—a subtle discomfort deep down inside. It would have been easy to overlook. I could have praised God and said that He was answering my prayers, but that is not what was going off in my spirit. I felt a warning. It wasn't loud. It wasn't a dream, vision, or eruptive prophetic experience. But it was a subdued sense that something wasn't quite right. I did not commit to anything, and left the meeting determined to pray. In the coming days, I sought the Lord and began to draw two conclusions. First, I realized that this minister was trying to dislodge me from my assigned place. He wasn't just trying to help me out of the goodness of his heart, he was trying to lure me away from the leader and ministry where God had planted me.

Let's discuss the second thing God highlighted to me: I came to understand that there was something dark in operation. I couldn't put my finger on it, and God didn't elaborate. I just knew I needed not to engage this person further. I knew that the Lord was adamantly warning me to stay away.

Emotional manipulation and its witchcraft of seduction will try to draw you away from where God wants you. It will attempt to create a breach in your submission to God-ordained leaders and places. We must realize that destiny has places connected to it. I was in the exact space where God had sent me to and my life was being changed daily. Part of that process was dying to my flesh so that I could live in God's purposes. I didn't know then how the Lord was going to use me. The level of surrender that He was calling me to was connected to my purpose. I had to give Him my full yes. We often fail to realize that the tests of today are preparing us for the exploits of tomorrow.

Seduction comes to destroy godly alignments. It comes to offer your flesh a quick promotion so that you can avoid the much-needed process of character development and sharpening. The enemy will also try to blind your eyes to his hidden schemes by speaking to your ambition. Ambition can be a poison to spiritual purpose. It will cause people to uproot themselves and bounce from place to place. I have seen it over and over. Ambition will bring forth a level of deception and attempt to convince a person that he or she is leaving a godly relationship based on a prophetic leading, when the truth is that the desire to be known, accepted, and relevant is really the root.

The devil is a skilled agent of deception. That test would not be my first or my last in spiritual seduction and destiny shortcuts. Every great champion will face the lure of moving before it's the proper time. It is dangerous because you learn so much in the waiting period! In the end, I left it with God, and never had another conversation about it. Many years later, that leader became embroiled in a horrendous scandal that destroyed his life and ministry. Many people were wounded. God knew it was coming and had rescued me. I wonder how many times we have been rescued by God's no! Thank Him for it and listen to it. Realize that the no is not a punishment, but a protection. The aim of seduction is to draw you away by false promises that appeal to your desires or your unhealed wounds.

"Now the Spirit expressly says that in latter times some will depart from the faith, giving heed to deceiving spirits and doctrines of demons" (1 Timothy 4:1). Seducing spirits want to lead you into a place of deception. They want to bind up your mind and affections. They speak to parts of you that may feel overlooked or underutilized. They can speak to wounds that have not been healed. This is the reason prayer is so vital! The Holy Spirit will create an inward check or give you a "grieving," an unease on the inside. It is a warning light from heaven, telling you that it is dangerous to proceed. This is God's protection for you arising in your spirit to keep you from error. God protected me, even though I didn't understand it at the time. It was all part of His plan.

Overcoming Emotional Manipulation

To keep yourself free from emotional manipulation and its subtle witchcraft, you must become sharp in your discernment. Not every "opportunity" comes from God! Not every "prophetic word" to you is born from a pure place. Not every "promise" comes without strings attached.

I want you to reflect on tests you have faced in the past. Have there been times in which you overrode God's no? Have you overlooked small warning signs only to become entangled in a toxic relationship or situation? Have you allowed human ambition and desire to become a dark weapon that uprooted you from a divine alignment?

If the answer to any of those questions is yes, then it is time to learn and grow. Reflect, repent, and determine to be more sensitive to God's no. Build a strong value for obedience to the Lord at all costs. This will help preserve you from emotional witchcraft. When you seek to please the Lord, live in spiritual and emotional health, and maintain your key covenant relationships (spouse, spiritual leaders or alignments, family, people whom the Lord has placed in your life for strategic purposes), the doorways for these demons will be closed.

As you look back on your life, do you recognize times when the enemy crept in because you ignored a warning? What lessons have you learned? How will you better face these challenges going forward? Do you realize that you have the ability to hear from God concerning all major decisions?

As a child of God, you are well equipped to recognize and overcome the plots of hell. Those plots may include nice people who say the right things, but there is something off in the realm of the spirit. One of the big keys of spiritual discernment is looking at the thing behind the thing. We need to practice discerning the "why"! *Why* are they offering help? What is the spirit that is motivating their actions? What troubling things do I feel, hear, sense, or see?

ooooooooooooo **LET'S REFLECT** ooooooooooooo

Grab a physical or digital journal and document your answers to the following questions:

1. As you read through this chapter, which people or situations did God bring to your mind? Describe those examples of emotional manipulation and witchcraft.
2. What is your "big why"? If you are not completely sure, what glimpses or insight has God given you about your purpose? (And don't be afraid to ask Him, if you have not!)
3. Draw a connection between your answers in questions 1 and 2. What strategies do you notice the enemy has used to derail you, based on who God called you to be? List them.
4. List two action steps found in this chapter that you can implement this week to pursue healing and freedom from emotional manipulation and witchcraft and its effects.

CHAPTER TWO

The Nice Church Lady

The young church planter was stunned. He could not believe what he was hearing! One of his most faithful new members was delivering him a mind-blowing ultimatum: make her copastor or she was out. How could she believe this was in order and okay? How could her husband go along with this sort of strong-arming approach?

The new pastor would have to make a firm decision. He would either cave to the control and pressure that he felt, or stand up to what he discerned was a manipulating spirit. What would the members think? How would his fledgling congregation navigate a sudden shift, and the departure of a key person? Was he discerning correctly? Was this normal? Do nice church ladies typically demand a pastoral position? All these emotions and ideas swirled in his mind as the church lady listed her résumé. Her husband stood nearly silent, with little engagement other than an occasional statement of support. The gauntlet had been thrown down, and a decision would have to be made.

To understand more fully what is happening here, let's return to the story's beginning. The church planter had been preaching in the area where the church lady lived when he had a vivid encounter with God. The Lord visited him and put a burden upon him for the territory. He discerned that the Lord was calling him and his wife to move into that territory and begin a church from scratch. This would be a tremendous leap of faith, but he was convinced that God was leading his decision.

> Now when they had gone through Phrygia and the region of Galatia, they were forbidden by the Holy Spirit to preach the word in Asia. After they had come to Mysia, they tried to go into Bithynia, but the Spirit did not permit them. So passing by Mysia, they came down to Troas. And a vision appeared to Paul in the night. A man of Macedonia stood and pleaded with him, saying, "Come over to Macedonia and help us." Now after he had seen the vision, immediately we sought to go to Macedonia, concluding that the Lord had called us to preach the gospel to them.
>
> Acts 16:6–10

Paul was ministering elsewhere when he had this night vision. As he pondered and prayed about the vision, he concluded that God was calling him to Macedonia. He then swiftly prepared and headed off on the assignment. In the same way, God calls His people to do extraordinary things in today's world! He gives dreams, visions, and promptings to reveal His will for them. The young church planter had experienced a very similar event. While driving home from preaching in the region, the power of God had come upon him so strongly that he had to pull off to the side of the road. He began to pray and intercede as the weight of the Lord's power rested on him. During that time of intercession, he deeply sensed that the Lord was calling him to build a work in that region. Just as Paul had to step out in faith, the pastor made a similar decision. He didn't know where to begin or where to seek help. But he understood that vision commands provision! When heaven speaks, resources and people will align. We often feel overwhelmed by the release of a mandate from heaven, but that's okay. It's God who will command the resources as we boldly stand in the vision. Vision is a source of divine strength and life. "Whoever walks blamelessly will be saved, but he who is perverse in his ways will suddenly fall. He who tills his land will have plenty of bread, but he who follows frivolity will have poverty enough!" (Proverbs 28:18–19).

Vision is a life-giving force because it is born of God. Anything connected to God brings life. When God releases a prophetic glimpse of the future, He reveals possibility and potential, and also releases His power to bring it to pass! The visionary connects people, resources, and places to the will of God. This is true not only in ministry but in every facet of life. As a child of God, vision is your birthright! God will lead you by His Spirit into His plans and purposes for you. As you step out in audacious faith, God's power will meet you.

It is critical to understand also that God-ordained assignments will also generate levels of warfare. Many times, we shrink back from heaven-sent assignments because we receive so much backlash. We must learn to recognize the warfare not as opposition, but as a confirmation, and be encouraged rather than discouraged. Satan attacks only what threatens him!

Vision also contains people and placement. God ordains destiny helpers to show up in our lives. He places them in the proper position. Warfare will try to come into our relationships, as well. I describe relationships as "God's transportation system." When He wants to get something into your life, He will bring the right relationship. Conversely, the enemy will do the same to get something wrong into your life! He will attempt to distract and defile you by bringing defiled relationships. We will unpack this more later—let's get back to the church lady and the church planter.

The lady had stepped up and offered to help with the new church in a major way. God provided a home where they could host home Bible studies. The lady was overseeing hospitality and seemed to be a major answer to prayer. She was quick to step up and ensure a flawless experience for those who would attend. From the perspective of the church planter, it appeared that God had sent a destiny helper. But under the surface, a storm was brewing! The woman had a desire to be seen and heard; her service was done with an agenda of unspoken expectations and impure spiritual motives. On the surface things seemed flawless, but part of the prophetic is about looking beneath the surface. It is the examination of the "why"! Too often we get stuck on the "what" and we don't look at the "why." Motive matters—and demons always operate with impure motives. One night, the young pastor and his wife both had a series of encounters and dreams related to the woman. It was a level of unexpected and intense warfare. What had been hidden was being revealed.

The Enemy's Exposure Through Dreams

"For there is nothing hidden which will not be revealed, nor has anything been kept secret but that it should come to light" (Mark 4:22). God will often uncover witchcraft and demonic operations through a dream. The immediate question might be, Why in our dreams instead of when we are awake? When it is dealing with people and relationships, it is often because we have human emotions that may be blocking our discernment. We love the people and feel close to them, so we cannot see what is lurking behind the scenes. Dreams from God supersede our emotions. They move beyond our own understanding and the mind of God is revealed in a dream or vision. The message is often concealed in symbolic dream language, which is the reason a gift of interpretation is needed. Discernment is for the mature—and remember, not everything that is discerned is to be spoken! If you have a prophetic gift, you must learn to "pray before you say." Some things are discerned for your prayer closet only. Others will have to be confronted in the right manner at the right time. Allowing God to lead you is critical in any discernment. Whenever you receive spiritual insight, wait for God to show spiritual solutions. To handle a spiritual insight in the flesh creates an abundance of trouble!

After the young church planter and his wife had those nighttime encounters, they took it to prayer. The Lord began to show them the operation of a Jezebel spirit. All the acts of kindness, favors, and service were being done with a hidden motive. Slowly, they began to rein the lady in and give her fewer and fewer opportunities. If you want to cause hidden demons to manifest, just place boundaries around them!

Demons despise authority. All acts of deliverance are acts of authority.

By the time the church lady's demands were made in that meeting, the young leaders were spiritually aware of the emotional manipulation, witchcraft, and hidden demons. They were resolved to obey God at any cost. Initially, they refused the demands. What followed is the normal protocol in situations with emotional witchcraft: a lot of outbursts, demands, and fits. There was a swell of emotions, along with accusations aimed to derail the fledgling church plant. The leaders remained rooted in the vision. The vision kept producing provision, and eventually the storm passed!

Emotional manipulation and witchcraft will try to trick you into believing lies. It will try to uproot your peace, confuse your discernment, and bombard your imagination with demonic lies. It is a lie in action! The answer is to pray, listen, and properly discern what is actually happening, and remain solid in the Word of God and in the mind of Christ. God's peace is the kind that supersedes both your circumstance and surroundings. That is the fruit of a mind planted in grace! God's grace upholds you in the times of adverse winds and attacks. There is grace for sonship, grace to build and plant, grace to prosper on every front, grace for right relationships at the right time, and grace to overcome all forms of demonic deception.

The harsh reality is that demons can come concealed in what appears to be "nice packaging." This is the reason we must not be led by our human mind and emotions, but by the Holy Spirit. We can easily miss the enemy's hidden operations. The church lady seemed kind, helpful, and like an answer to prayer, but the reality was that she came with an evil agenda! All emotional manipulation and emotional witchcraft are rooted in a desire. The person is doing what they're doing to fulfill their desire to dominate another. This is what must be adequately discerned to avoid a shipwreck.

"This is the message which we have heard from Him and declare to you, that God is light and in Him is no darkness at all. If we say that we have fellowship with Him, and walk in darkness, we lie and do not practice the truth" (1 John 1:5–6). Deception does its best work under the cover of darkness. The enemy lives in darkness and demon powers operate undercover. Emotional manipulation and witchcraft often take place through people and situations that you fail to discern. Their actions and words will be very appealing, to try to persuade you! In most cases, there is an internal concern that you notice, but then override. You may be in a conversation where someone is making promises, assuring you of a favorable outcome, yet you feel this nagging unrest in the pit of your stomach. Don't let your mind talk you out of what your spirit is assessing! Pray, listen, discern!

"He has delivered us from the power of darkness and conveyed us into the kingdom of the Son of His love" (Colossians 1:13). According to *Strong's Concordance*, one meaning of the Greek word for *power* used in this verse is "jurisdiction."[1] Another translation uses the word as *domain*. If we think of it in that manner, we are thinking of a kingdom and place of rule. When we are born again, we are brought out from under the rule of darkness and into the light and revelation of Christ Jesus. Demon entities hide their wicked maneuvers in the domain of darkness, under the cover of night. When God illuminates our hearts with His revelation, we see in the unseen, and the light of God brings much-needed exposure.

I often tell prophetic people that this is the reason why the enemy wars against them so strongly! Their sight, their understanding, and their discernment threaten him. He knows that they will unveil his operation and render him inoperable. The enemy's plots must remain hidden for them to succeed. When we see and discern what he is doing, we can then effectively combat his operations.

The Enemy's Exposure by a "Knowing"

One way that we discern demons wrapped in cute packages is by a "knowing." This is an often-overlooked method of God's Spirit leading us. We fail to realize the importance of this function, because we are accustomed to thinking of leading as dreams, visions, or the spoken voice of God. All those operations come into play when we deal with discernment, but our born-again spirit person sometimes just knows that something is off. This can feel like an inner impression, a "gut feeling," or a subtle sense that something is wrong. Many times, when I experienced this, I was unsure of the root. I couldn't explain it well; I just felt, perceived, or knew it.

"And Jesus, immediately knowing in Himself that power had gone out of Him, turned around in the crowd and said, 'Who touched my clothes?'" (Mark 5:30). This is the story of Jesus healing the woman with the issue of blood. It says that He knew in Himself that virtue or power had gone out. According to *Strong's Concordance*, the word for *knowing* there means to "perceive," "know accurately," and "to understand."[2] At that moment, He didn't necessarily have a vision or hear the Father speaking to Him. He had an insight and perception. Many people miss this kind of discernment. There are times in which the Lord shows us something about an individual or situation that is so vivid that it is undeniable, yet at other times it is simply a knowing. We need to be in tune with our born-again spirit person and the leading of the Holy Spirit not to overlook His messages to us.

Proverbs 20:27 says, "The spirit of man is the lamp of the Lord." This means that God will illuminate our inner person to reveal to us what needs to be known. You may be in the middle of a conversation and have an inner impression that something is not right. You may suddenly sense and perceive there is a warning. When this happens, stop and pay attention to what your spirit man is perceiving. You don't want to miss vital communication from heaven intended to warn and protect you.

One of the primary ways the Holy Spirit leads us is through such an inward witness. We must learn to recognize it. It is not difficult! When we have a "check" in our spirit, this feels to our emotions a little like when our car flashes a caution light! It may be a sense of being unsettled. It's not always a voice saying, "Don't do this," or "Don't go on that trip." It may just be an inward knowing that we shouldn't do something or go somewhere. Truthfully, if we look back on some of our biggest mistakes, we can see that we could have avoided them if we simply listened to what we were perceiving through this kind of knowing, this the inner witness.

Peace as a Profound Indicator

As we learn to yield to the inner witness, we must recognize that peace is a profound indicator of the will of God in our lives. When we obey God, and then follow His will, we will experience a deep and abiding peace that transcends our understanding. The peace of God can act as an "umpire," helping to provide necessary guidance in our decisions and daily affairs.

We should know when there is both the presence of peace and the absence of it. In Colossians 3:15, the apostle Paul instructs us, "And let the peace of God rule in your hearts, to which also you were called in one body; and be thankful." God's peace is evidence that we are on the right track! Conversely, the absence of peace indicates that something is amiss. The Amplified Bible Classic Edition of that verse states it this way:

> And let the peace (soul harmony which comes) from Christ rule (act as umpire continually) in your hearts [deciding and settling with finality all questions that arise in your minds, in that peaceful state] to which as [members of Christ's] one body you were also called [to live]. And be thankful (appreciative), [giving praise to God always].

As we pray and align with heaven, a supernatural and abiding peace overtakes us. This is the atmosphere of God's Kingdom!

> Do not fret or have any anxiety about anything, but in every circumstance and in everything, by prayer and petition (definite requests), with thanksgiving, continue to make your

wants known to God. And God's peace [shall be yours, that tranquil state of a soul assured of its salvation through Christ, and so fearing nothing from God and being content with its earthly lot of whatever sort that is, that peace] which transcends all understanding shall garrison and mount guard over your hearts and minds in Christ Jesus.

Philippians 4:6–7 AMPC

When we are in step with the Spirit and in partnership with the Lord, there is an abundance of peace. When we are thinking about inner knowing, peace is a tremendous part of the process. God will show us the way to go by the presence of His peace. God's peace is not based in logic or circumstance. You can enjoy the peace of God in the middle of a life crisis. There is a profound sense of well-being and assurance that comes from being in His will. Jesus Himself reassured His disciples in John 14:27, saying, "Peace I leave with you, My peace I give to you; not as the world gives do I give to you. Let not your heart be troubled, neither let it be afraid."

Being led by the Holy Spirit is a promise to God's sons and daughters:

For all who are being led by the Spirit of God, these are sons and daughters of God. For you have not received a spirit of slavery leading to fear again, but you have received a spirit of adoption as sons and daughters by which we cry out, "Abba! Father!" The Spirit Himself testifies with our spirit that we are children of God.

Romans 8:14–16 NASB

We are not left without divine guidance and insight in the affairs of life. This is relational. It is the fruit of walking with God and should be the normal way of life for all believers.

Living Out of Your New Nature

How can we avoid being duped by a person who masquerades as a helper, when in fact the person is sent to ensnare us? One key is learning to live out of your new nature. "And put on the new nature (the regenerate self) created in God's image, [Godlike] in true righteousness and holiness" (Ephesians 4:24 AMPC). When you were born again, your spirit person was made in the image and likeness of God. This means that your spirit is able to think like God, move like God, and desires to please God.

Hearing and knowing the voice of God should be commonplace for believers, but it is foreign to many! This is for two reasons: First, many believers have not been properly taught regarding their identity. They don't know who they are, and so the enemy keeps them living far beneath their means. Second, they don't recognize all the ways that God can and does speak to them. This is necessary learning if we want to be led by God's Spirit. He is always speaking, but His voice is multifaceted.

You have been given spiritual senses to receive communication from God! Just as your physical man has senses, so does your spirit man. You have spiritual eyes that can see, spiritual ears that can hear, and senses of taste, touch, and smell as well. God's voice speaks in many ways.

Prophets in the Old Testament were called seers: "Formerly in Israel, when a man went to inquire of God, he spoke thus: 'Come, let us go to the seer'; for he who is now called a prophet was formerly called a seer" (1 Samuel 9:9). Seers were ones who processed the voice of God in visual form. In Ephesians 1, Paul prays for the church at Ephesus to have their spiritual eyes opened. This means that he was asking God to raise up a generation of believers who could adequately see with spiritual sight. Spiritual sight includes pictures, symbols, dreams, and visions. One way that God can warn you is through the realm of sight. I like to say it this way: It is the voice of God, but coming across your spiritual eyes as a vivid image in order to deliver a critical message.

"He who has an ear, let him hear what the Spirit says to the churches" (Revelation 2:7). We can hear the voice of God because we have spiritual ears. There are different levels of auditory communication. One of the most stunning ways God speaks to our spiritual ears is through His audible voice. We hear Him in an audible voice like that of another person speaking to us. A more common way that God speaks to our spiritual ears is through His still, small voice. We hear it with our spiritual ears, but it requires tuning in.

Once, as a young minister, I sat in a meeting with certain leaders who wanted me to affiliate my ministry with them. They were offering me economic support and assistance. At the time, I was launching out on another level by faith; their partnership could have made a big difference. As I sat there listening, everything they were saying sounded so good! In the middle of the meeting, I heard the word *Lies!* When I heard this, I was shocked, but it was crystal clear. I heard this in my inner man. I began to ponder what I heard, and I knew the Lord was showing me not to take their offer. I knew that there was deception involved. My wife was in the meeting also and heard something very similar. That word saved me from heaps of trouble! Years later, their ministry was embroiled in controversy and crisis. God had spared me because I listened to His voice!

Here is one of several Scriptures that mention smell in a spiritual sense: "And walk in love, as Christ also has loved us and given Himself for us, an offering and a sacrifice to God for a sweet-smelling aroma" (Ephesians 5:2). I have seen times in deep worship experiences in which people reported a beautiful aroma. While this experience was so vivid to some people in the room, others didn't smell anything. For those who did experience the aroma, it was a confirmation of the presence of the Lord. I would suggest that this is the discerning of spirits in operation, allowing people to recognize the sweet presence of Jesus. Conversely, I have had experiences with demonized people in which I smelled a foul odor. I have known many people who encountered this, and have come to realize that demons carry a spiritual stench. One way we may discern this is the activation of the sense of spiritual smell. It is a tool of discernment. Not everyone will experience it, but for those who do, it becomes a confirmation from the Lord.

This verse reveals that the word of the Lord carries a sweet taste: "How sweet are Your words to my taste, sweeter than honey to my mouth!" (Psalm 119:103). This speaks of our spiritual sense of taste. The presence of the Lord and of demons can be revealed at times through this spiritual sense.

We can often recognize demons and angels when we feel their presence. We might not hear or see anything, but we feel their presence. As we saw earlier, Jesus felt and perceived the release of virtue: "Immediately the fountain of her blood was dried up, and she felt in her body that she was healed of the affliction. And Jesus, immediately knowing in Himself that power had gone out of Him, turned around in the crowd and said, 'Who touched my clothes?'" (Mark 5:29–30). Notice that the woman also immediately felt power enter her body and realized that God had healed her of her infirmity.

"God Thoughts"

You can also receive impressions, thoughts, and subtle revelations by the mind of the Spirit: "Now He who searches the hearts knows what the mind of the Spirit is, because He makes intercession for the saints according to the will of God" (Romans 8:27). There are many ways God can direct our paths through the mind of the Spirit. One way is what I call "God thoughts." They are illuminations that come like thoughts, but are born of the Spirit.

We also may have impressions, which are almost like a feeling but they are spiritual, not mental. When you have an impression about something or someone, you know that it is deeper than a thought. As we discussed earlier, you have an inward knowing. This is when you just know something by the Spirit and there is no escaping it. It is not something that came to you through a tremendous encounter, but just through a simple knowing.

Another manifestation is the leading of the Lord. This operates as a deep desire and prompting to move in a specific direction. When we are prompted, it becomes an unction that we cannot escape. We know that we are being directed to act in a particular area.

I could write many more chapters on the complexity of God's voice. There are so many ways that God can and does talk to His people. We have just scratched the surface, but these are brief insights into understanding and embracing God's multifaceted voice and leading in the daily affairs of our lives. Emotional manipulation and witchcraft are going to occur at their most effective levels by being disguised. This is the reason we must be diligent to pay attention to the checks, warnings, and leadings that the Lord gives us to keep us from being duped by the enemy.

○○○○○○○○○○○ LET'S REFLECT ○○○○○○○○○○○

1. Have you had a dream from God that gave insight into witchcraft or demonic operation in your life? If so, describe it.
2. When was the last time that God gave you a "knowing" or a "check" about something? How did you respond to it? What can you do to improve your response in the future?
3. Peace is a profound indicator of the will of God in our lives. Make a list of connections and situations where the peace of God has been a confirmation in your life.
4. What are some ways that you hear God speaking to you? List two ways that you can sharpen and become more confident in your ability to hear and obey Him.

CHAPTER THREE

The Purpose of Godly Relationships

Life was never meant to be lived alone. We are all living, loving, and growing daily. Friendships, family relationships, and kingdom relationships are intended to be a rich and fulfilling part of our lives. They can also be extremely challenging! We need to remember that we are dust! We carry God's divine nature, but it is housed in a clay pot: "But we have this treasure in earthen vessels, that the excellence of the power may be of God and not of us" (2 Corinthians 4:7).

At times, our struggle between our God-given destiny and our own human weaknesses can be intense. We need to pull back the lens to see and remember that humanity is part of who we are. We have limits, appetites, and challenges. We also have beautiful and wonderful experiences as human beings. We feel deeply, live with passion, and experience life in high definition. These realities impact not only a person's individual journey with God but also each relationship and connection.

To fully appreciate and successfully enjoy enriching relationships, we need a strong revelation of the grace of God.

Without understanding the grace of God and His abundant love toward us, we can become extremely critical and judgmental. This will create shame-based relationships that diminish the people in our lives, instead of enriching them.

Without a revelation of the grace of God, we tend to judge ourselves and others using a dangerous combination of law, judgment, and anger. We then view God's attitude toward us as one of anger and bitterness, instead of one of love and acceptance. This creates a mindset and environment of internal unrest that bleeds into and onto all our relationships. We wonder why we can't seem to have fruitful and meaningful relationships, but many times it's because we lack a revelation of grace.

Supernatural Bonds

"Now when he had finished speaking to Saul, the soul of Jonathan was knit to the soul of David, and Jonathan loved him as his own soul" (1 Samuel 18:1). Jonathan was the son of King Saul and in the line of succession to the throne. David, however, was God's choice for the next king. These two men met at a critical time in their lives and in the life of the nation of Israel. God supernaturally knit their hearts together in an uncommon fashion. In many ways, their friendship did not make sense. Why would Jonathan so deeply love David, when his father was at odds with him? There was a supernatural bond in their hearts toward each other. They met as strangers but ended as brothers.

Many times, when God sends people into your life for an assignment, there's an unusual flow of love toward them that may supersede your own human understanding. Jonathan and David, the future king of Israel, shared a deep and loyal friendship. Despite Jonathan being the natural heir to the throne, he supported David and recognized God's anointing on David's life. Jonathan honored who David was. Their friendship was a brotherhood characterized by mutual respect, loyalty, and sacrifice. It is one of the relationships in the Bible that illustrates the importance of godly friendships and the role they play in the unfolding of our kingdom assignments.

People often ask me how to identify God's leading concerning friendships and kingdom relationships. One thing I look for is favor! When God wants me to connect with someone, He will place a desire in my heart. In other words, He favors them in my own heart. Again, it is a divine flow. This divine flow becomes not only a confirmation but also a catalyst for a deepening relationship.

In other words, it's neither difficult nor challenging to have the relationship. There is an easy flow! I can see the work of grace concerning the relationship by the flow in my own heart toward the other individual and the reciprocity of grace from them back to me. These are some of my favorite relationships, the ones which organically unfold. When they first begin, I may not recognize the tremendous level of impact they'll have on my life, but favor spurs me on to continue the investigation.

Learn to Follow the Favor

"For You are the glory of their strength, and in Your favor our horn is exalted" (Psalm 89:17). According to Webster's online dictionary, the word *favor* means "to show partiality to or to prefer."[1] When God begins to do something in your life, He will cause you to be preferred. You will be preferred to be set in certain spaces with certain people who are destiny connections.

Years ago, I had a deep passion for God's work and had seen a much older preacher minister. This man moved with power, both in his preaching ministry and in his laying hands on people for miracles and impartation. Something in me was drawn to what was upon him. I have found that the Lord will bring certain people into our lives who speak to our future destiny. This pattern has been repeated often in my life, throughout my journey. When God does this, I recognize His purpose.

The Lord opened a door for me to get to know this preacher up close. He poured into me by mentoring and spending time with me. Eventually, he invited me into spaces of ministry that exceeded my expectations. I vividly remember being invited on a large ministry trip with him and a huge team to another nation. Everyone on the trip was part of the same organization except for me and a couple of other guys. Very soon, many other participants were asking me how I got to go on that trip. They were dumbfounded, because it didn't make any sense.

The truth is, they were correct! My answer was simple: favor. God had favored me and given this preacher a love for me. He was giving me a front-row seat to learn and grow by being close to this man of God. My position was one of destiny, and favor was the catalyst that got me there. That preacher has gone on to be with the Lord now, but I will never forget the impact he had on me. He was vital in my development and growth during a season in which I was searching for answers. Only God could have brought him to me. God knew that I would not mishandle the relationship.

"And so find favor and high esteem in the sight of God and man" (Proverbs 3:4). We need favor with God and man! Man is often the chosen instrument to bless us, increase our reach, and release critical wisdom to us. Favor is the key that unlocks relational doors. It's vital that you learn to follow the favor. Take note of it and maximize it. Favor swells in our hearts toward the people God has chosen for our lives. When we are to be connected, it is not difficult. We want to be in the presence of that person. There is a heavenly flow on the relationship.

A Lack of Divine Flow

Throughout my years of leadership, I have had people enter my life who were difficult to connect with. It wasn't just timing or personality differences. There was just a lack of divine flow. One very gifted young leader came into my life claiming that she needed alignment and help in development. Everything about her was hard to deal with. She demanded loads of attention with little results. She frequently ignored my counsel, choosing instead to listen to others. When we would try to pin down times for necessary conversations, it was always challenging.

Now, let me state this: It was more than busyness and schedule! It is not wise to evaluate a kingdom relationship based only on natural matters. It is much deeper than that. As this relationship unfolded, this young leader lit several troubling relational fires in my ministry circle. She talked too much, especially about other people. She had a short fuse and said negative things.

The issue for me was that I could clearly see how gifted she was and what a major weapon she could be with the right mentorship. But I also began to realize that I was not that mentor! The relationship created nothing but drama. My spiritual and emotional batteries were drained when I had to have long conversations with her; I didn't see a powerful impact from the relationship. Issues and problems abounded. Eventually, I had to do a heart evaluation, and I realized that there was a lack of favor in the relationship. I had to have a hard conversation with her, and release her from my circle. My heart was grieved, but my life was blessed.

There are some people whose entry into your life really blesses you! Then there are other people who incite a praise party when they exit. Can we just stop a moment and have a praise party for those divine exits? Come on, you know that you have been blessed by some departures!

Shifting Seasons Shift Your Circle

"Two are better than one, because they have a good reward for their labor. For if they fall, one will lift up his companion. But woe to him that is alone when he falls, for he has no one to help him up" (Ecclesiastes 4:9–10). When the right people come into your life, they lift you up. It doesn't mean that they won't say tough things at times, but their motive is your well-being. They may confront or correct you, but they do so as an ally. Their presence in your life is a sustaining and maturing force. Many times, when God was shifting my season, He would also shift my circle. Have you ever experienced a huge shift in your squad? If you are not praying and really looking at it through a spiritual lens, it can be very disheartening.

But once you learn to identify season shifts and relationship shifts, you'll see God's handiwork in action.

Years ago, I experienced one of my most challenging, yet rewarding, circle shifts. I had been pondering the next steps of my prophetic destiny after receiving several profound prophetic words that spoke of both promotion and shifting. Suddenly, new doors began to open in rapid succession. It was so fast, I began to seek the Lord about it. I will never forget what He told me. He said, *I have announced you! When I announce you, doors will open that no man can close.*

I was elated by all that God was doing in my life. Dreams were being fulfilled and opportunities were granted. During that promotion, I made a major transition in my ministry assignment. I went from pastoring and leading local campuses to overseeing and traveling. God was moving in profound ways.

But issues began to arise. People I had walked with for many years began to grumble. There were secret and not-so-secret complaints. Conversations didn't seem to resolve the problems. The more questions I asked, the deeper the complaints ran. The season ended with some extremely painful exits, and relationships that broke off suddenly, and with many tears. My mind swirled with questions: *How could the very people who prayed with me for these doors to open now be offended when I walked through them? Why did they seem unable to celebrate my new assignment and season? Where did I miss it? Where did they miss it?*

But in this challenging season, new people started showing up! God blessed me with some people who not only understood my pivot but also partnered with it. They were excited, on board, and ready to help. It would have been very easy to sink down in despair by looking only at the exits; I also needed to see and appreciate the entries. During this time, God brought a new friend into my life, an accomplished minister, entrepreneur, and author with experience. Suddenly God opened tremendous doors. The experience was not without pain over lost relationships; there had been a once-tight inner circle who prayed daily for the ministry and knew God was going to expand it. However, when expansion came, some folks in that circle were offended! This sounded eerily familiar.

I realized it was a pattern. Sometimes, when new levels open and new doors swing wide, relationships shift. God will release people who are limited in their perspective and refuse to grow. He will also bring people into your life who are well equipped for your new and next season. They are purpose partners who are ready to "take the mountain" with you.

Things around you can be a bit fragile during times of transition. Also, some emotional manipulation and witchcraft may attempt to creep in because people are uncomfortable with your growth. But you were never intended to stay at the same level all your life. God takes you into new seasons and guides you through new doors. This can create intimidation in the hearts of people who are uncomfortable with your growth. They will usually lash out at you, accuse you, or gossip about you. They do these things to get you to submit to their desire to abandon growth for their own comfort. It is manipulation at its highest!

I experienced an abundance of this kind of behavior during that shifting season. Looking back, it was one of the most challenging seasons I had experienced, but I refused to cave to the pressure and opinions of others. I was determined to keep growing. No one in your life has a right to halt or limit your growth. Growth is necessary and normal. Never feel guilty for growing, and never compromise your growth to satisfy others. Don't cater to the opinions of people who settle for less when they could be pressing on toward the goal. Don't feel bad that God brought some new people for your next season. Love everyone, but follow God!

Core Principles of Godly Relationships

Relationships are God's transportation system. When He wants to bring things to you, He will often do so through relationships. They are divine instruments in your life. Let's look at a few core principles of healthy and meaningful spiritual relationships: *connection*, *proximity*, *trust*, *accountability*, *support*, and *rebuke*.

The first core principle is *connection*. You cannot benefit from a relationship if you are unwilling to connect. A relationship is a connection. When God aligns two people, they need to be intentional about connecting.

The next principle is *proximity*. You need to create space in your life for a relationship. It demands that you get up close. This may be difficult if you are still recovering from past trauma or issues; that's the reason emotional healing is a necessary ingredient in your relational journey.

Another principle in a healthy and meaningful spiritual relationship is *trust*. It is very difficult to have any meaningful relationship without an element of trust. Look at the trust and proximity between the apostle Paul and Timothy:

Then came he to Derbe and Lystra: and, behold, a certain disciple was there, named Timothy, the son of a certain Jewish woman who believed, but his father was a Greek: he was well spoken of by the brethren who were at Lystra and Iconium. Paul wanted to have him go on with him. And he took him and circumcised him because of the Jews who were in that region, for they all knew that his father was Greek. And as they went through the cities, they delivered to them the decrees to keep, which were determined by the apostles and elders at Jerusalem.

Acts 16:1–4

Paul recognized that God was calling him to mentor and disciple Timothy. Conversely, Timothy discerned the importance of his relationship with Paul. Paul checked into Timothy's reputation and character so that he knew what Timothy was like. (We can save ourselves many issues by checking past behaviors and testimonies before jumping headlong into certain relationships.)

Paul then asked Timothy to be circumcised—as an adult male! This was not an easy thing. Sometimes, leaders will ask us to do things that stretch us. While Paul did not require this of every spiritual son, he did of Timothy. He based his decision on Timothy's cultural background, where they would be traveling, and the assignment at hand. Timothy trusted Paul, and said yes to the pain! This was a huge leap of faith. Timothy stayed close to Paul, which may not have been convenient for him, but he trusted Paul as he took Timothy not into a classroom, but to a mission field.

Leaders, we often fail at leadership relationships when we think the mentee should dictate the tone and pace of the mentor. The mentor sets that rhythm. When God has placed leaders in my life, it was up to me to get in proximity by listening to and reading their teaching. I needed to go to their gatherings. This is how I related to their mantle and calling. In the first church I led, I would have people who rarely attended services come for counsel and wisdom. Many times, the things they were struggling with had been addressed in the teachings that they missed. I learned through the years to pay attention to people's hunger by their attendance. The truth is, we prioritize what we value. If we value a relationship, we will create the time and space for it.

A further principle of godly relationships is *accountability*. Whether it is a close friend, a spouse, or a leader, that person can help you be accountable in vital areas of your life. God sends people to you who will say the difficult things, help you prioritize your growth, and help you stay on track with God. Accountability is a major part of our personal and spiritual growth. Without it, we can remain stuck. Healthy accountability does not come with accusation or manipulation, but with your best interest at heart. It is very dangerous to surround ourselves with people who affirm the worst parts of us and won't speak up when we miss the mark! We need people who believe in our destiny strongly enough to remind us of the godly standards we have set in our lives.

Godly relationships also provide *support*. They help bring support spiritually, emotionally, and personally. The right people in your life act as a guard and garrison. Jonathan was a support to David. Timothy was a support to Paul. When we think of spiritual assignments, we also need to think about divine alignments. God will align us with the right people for the right assignments. "Therefore encourage (admonish, exhort) one another and edify (strengthen and build up) one another, just as you are doing" (1 Thessalonians 5:11 AMPC). The right relationships bring encouragement at critical intersections of destiny.

Let's be honest: When we take big leaps of faith, the enemy often attacks, and the unknown can be a scary place to navigate alone. We need people who will lift us up and help us build our future. The right friends and alignments can help to make our destiny. A lot of people fall into the trap of the enemy's emotional manipulation because they don't have anyone healthy in their corner cheering them on. Everyone needs people who strengthen them and build them up.

Another principle of divine relationships is loving *rebuke*. Kingdom relationships will bring correction, both from peers and from mentors or overseers. This kind of rebuke does not come from a place of mean-spirited nastiness; it comes from a desire to see us rise and live to our full potential. "Open rebuke is better than love carefully concealed. Faithful are the wounds of a friend, but the kisses of an enemy are deceitful" (Proverbs 27:5–6). When a faithful friend rebukes us, it is because of love. That friend desires to see us grow, so the person informs us of what they see in us that may hinder our growth. Often, we run from those hard conversations because we may feel triggered, based on painful past experiences. But in this case, it is important to make the distinction between toxic love and healthy love and allow yourself to receive the healthy love that comes by way of correction.

One of the charges that Paul gave to Timothy as a leader was to issue rebuke: "I charge you therefore before God and the Lord Jesus Christ, who will judge the living and the dead at His appearing and His kingdom: Preach the word! Be ready in season and out of season. Convince, rebuke, exhort, with all longsuffering and teaching" (2 Timothy 4:1–2). The word *rebuke* here can mean "to admonish, forbid, and to charge." Strong leaders are willing to bring correction and confront areas in our lives that may cause us to miss the mark. One of the things I appreciated most about my spiritual father was his willingness to say difficult things to me. It never felt good in the moment, but as I reflected upon it, I realized that it was for my good. He saw both my potential and my blind spots. He didn't mind hurting my feelings in the moment, because he could see where I was going long-term. He has gone on to be with the Lord, and I greatly miss him!

Relationships as a Mirror

The right relationships will help strengthen and sharpen you. They will refine your character and gift. We need people who refuse to allow us to be dull. We need to be sharp in the realm of the spirit and we need to be strong in our purpose and character. Relationships can act as a mirror in our lives, reflecting the depths of our hearts and revealing areas that need growth, healing, and strengthening.

The human connections we form with others can be challenging, fragile, and even frustrating at times. But that is part of the beauty of it. Many times, I have complained about a relationship, placing blame on another person, only to have the Lord point back to my own heart. This is the "mirror" I am referring to. God may send us a difficult person so that we learn to love. (And maybe that person isn't difficult at all; he or she just sees the world differently than we do!)

This is one of the things I find so fascinating about spiritual gifts, ministry gifts, and service gifts. Jesus has invested various portions of Himself into individuals. They have unique pain points and passions! When you get them all together, they can dialogue and debate, even when they're convinced that their perspective is right and others wrong. The reality is, it is often just a different lens through which we are invited to see the world.

Jesus masterfully connects us and commands us to love one another, regardless of our differences. Through the dynamics of various interactions, we become aware of our fears, shortcomings, emotional issues, and unhealed wounds we might not have recognized otherwise. This mirroring effect challenges us to confront and address these aspects, leading us on a path of deep and lasting personal and spiritual development. As Proverbs 27:17 states, "As iron sharpens iron, so a man sharpens the countenance of his friend." The relationships we nurture are instrumental in sharpening and refining our character, prompting us to become healthier people and more effective kingdom ambassadors.

Relationships as Destiny Connections

Relationships also serve as vital destiny connections, through which God orchestrates His plans and purposes in our lives. He brings individuals into our journey not only for companionship but also to release something significant to us. These divine connections can spur our spiritual growth, bring necessary encouragement, and empower the release of God's blessing and wisdom.

Relationships also uncover buried and hidden wounds, bringing them to the surface not just for the sake of exposure but for healing and deliverance. This process, though sometimes painful, is critical for our well-being and wholeness. As we allow God to work through our relationships, we find ourselves being healed, restored, and equipped for greater kingdom exploits.

When you begin to understand the necessity and validity of relationships, you can start to understand why the enemy attacks them so strongly. When the right people show up in your life, hell gets nervous. Because of the power of right relationships, the enemy will do all he can to send the wrong people! This is where emotional manipulation and witchcraft become such foul tools of the enemy. He will send unhealed and demonized people to distract, discourage, and delay you. He wants to keep you stuck in the trap of strife and confusion so that he can keep you away from your destiny.

Don't be surprised by the presence of toxic relationships. Think of it like mining for gold; sometimes you sift through the dirt and grime to get to those nuggets. You may encounter people who you thought were being sent to bless you, only to realize that they were not heaven's best for you. As you heal and grow, your discernment about relationships will grow. You will learn to recognize patterns of bad or messy behavior. This equips you to close the gates to the enemy and to build wise connections with the right people God has sent you.

Stewarding Spiritual Relationships

It is also vital to realize that relationships need to be categorized, prioritized, and defined. There are levels of relationships in our lives. For example, in the life of a married person, the highest human relationship is with a spouse. All others take a back seat. That relationship is to be guarded, because it's a relationship in which the two become one! When we examine the relational dynamics with our immediate family, we notice that there are differing obligations to our children and parents than there are to others.

Relationships with a spiritual leader such as a pastor, mentor, or other godly leader also carry a different purpose. Because various relationships have differing purposes, it is critical that we properly understand and define a relationship so that we are aligned with its purpose and have reasonable expectations. Not doing this can shipwreck the purpose of the relationship. We can sabotage these kinds of relationships by expecting a friendship, and thus create a false expectation that will disappoint us. A leader is placed in our lives to grow us, empower us, impart to us, and equip us. That is different from the role of a friend.

I want you to pause and ponder these questions: Have you matured in the stewardship of your relationships? Have you learned to properly identify various roles in your life and then set your expectations accordingly? Do you default to blaming others anytime there is a relational conflict? Do you run from conflict?

We must realize that sharpening requires some conflict. Maturity will mean disagreement, because each of us brings a different perspective to the table. If we all saw the world the same way, then we would miss living out our purpose and making our mark! God places people around us to impact our lives and be part of our journey. Meaningful relationships are not perfect and still get messy, but that is part of the process. As we grow and mature, we will realize the need for healthy relationships and the danger of unhealthy ones. This foundation will help us to spot and quickly reject manipulation and emotional witchcraft. The healthier we become, the less vulnerable we will be to these demonic ploys.

∘∘∘∘∘∘∘∘∘∘∘∘ **LET'S REFLECT** ∘∘∘∘∘∘∘∘∘∘∘∘

1. Identify two areas in your life where God has given you favor. This can be in friendship, in ministry, in business, or in other areas.
2. List an action step for each area of favor where you can honor or maximize the connection.
3. Which core principle of godly relationships stood out to you the most? Why?
4. Your relationships need to be categorized, prioritized, and defined. Consider each relationship in your life and apply these three necessities to each one.

CHAPTER FOUR

Manipulation Strategies Exposed

> Clothe yourselves therefore, as God's own chosen ones (His own picked representatives), [who are] purified and holy and well-beloved [by God Himself, by putting on behavior marked by] tenderhearted pity and mercy, kind feeling, a lowly opinion of yourselves, gentle ways, [and] patience [which is tireless and long-suffering, and has the power to endure whatever comes, with good temper]. Be gentle and forbearing with one another and, if one has a difference (a grievance or complaint) against another, readily pardoning each other; even as the Lord has [freely] forgiven you, so must you also [forgive]. And above all these [put on] love and enfold yourselves with the bond of perfectness [which binds everything together completely in ideal harmony].
>
> Colossians 3:12–14 AMPC

When the Holy Spirit is truly leading us, we begin to take on more and more of His nature. He illuminates the areas of our hearts that need to change so that we look more like the Father. He gives us insight into how we can align with His ways. He lights up the pathways that we are to travel. He causes the love of God to live big in us! This is one of the markers of a surrendered life. Love will require us to do difficult things. It is impossible to really walk with God without taking on portions of His nature and characteristics. One of the most challenging things to comprehend with our human limitations is God's unqualified love toward us. You may say, "Well, what do you mean by unqualified?" I mean, God loved us before we ever responded to Him in love. This is unfathomable to the human mind.

We tend to love one another based on what we do for each other. This is a (dysfunctional) transactional form of "love." But the presence of God in our lives draws us closer to the one who is love itself. God doesn't just walk in love, He *is* love. As we journey deeper into His heart, we journey into a heart filled with love. It's not a conditional love or a love contingent upon our actions or reactions, but one that is predicated on His very nature—kind, gentle, all-knowing, and all-powerful. Even with His mind-blowing capacity to understand and know all things, including our frailty and weakness, He has an unwavering love toward us. In our ongoing relationship with Him, we are apprehended by love. His love arrests us and causes us to stand still in awe and wonder of who He is and what He does. We find ourselves gazing with astonishment at the mystery of His love. It is the presence of His unchanging, unwavering love that sets our hearts free from shame and condemnation, and then causes us to soar!

> Love endures long and is patient and kind; love never is envious nor boils over with jealousy, is not boastful or vainglorious, does not display itself haughtily.

> It is not conceited (arrogant and inflated with pride); it is not rude (unmannerly) and does not act unbecomingly. Love (God's love in us) does not insist on its own rights or its own way, for it is not self-seeking; it is not touchy or fretful or resentful; it takes no account of the evil done to it [it pays no attention to a suffered wrong]. It does not rejoice at injustice and unrighteousness, but rejoices when right and truth prevail. Love bears up under anything and everything that comes, is ever ready to believe the best of every person, its hopes are fadeless under all circumstances, and it endures everything [without weakening].
>
> 1 Corinthians 13:4–7 AMPC

Love doesn't keep score, is not easily offended, and extends mercy toward others. This is a love deeper than human ability! It is God working through us and in us. It is God guiding and leading us. The deeper we go in God, the stronger the work of love will be in our lives.

Love Versus Manipulation

God once taught me a valuable lesson about walking in love. I was young in the ministry and full of zeal. I often thought it was my job to let people know where they were falling short. (Can you relate to that at all? You know, we prophetic types can sometimes be hard to deal with!) I was having a heated disagreement with another staff member at the ministry where I worked. In my mind, this person was flighty. She had a track record of bouncing from ministry to ministry, and had several failed relationships. I honestly couldn't understand why she was even working at the ministry. As our disagreement grew more heated, I rebuked her with my razor-sharp tongue. I walked away from the encounter feeling justified because, after all, I was right! (Don't judge me. You know you have had your moments too; I am just being extremely honest here.) The young me needed a lot of work, but he got an A+ for exuberance, and in this instance he was exuberantly expressing his disagreement with no grace at all!

Later that day, the Lord spoke to me and I was astounded. He told me that I needed to go and apologize to the lady for how I handled her. I began to plead with Him, telling Him how she was wrong in what she had done in the ministry. I told Him that if I apologized, she would think she was right! I was God's professional scorekeeper—and that is a sure sign of a lack of grace. If you are a champion scorekeeper, you are lacking grace. As I argued my case with God, He told me that this coworker's actions were out of order, but that my heart was wrong. He told me my apology was about me and my heart more than it was about her. I saw His point and yielded. I apologized to her and learned a valuable lesson about the grace of God.

Particularly in the lives of prophetic people and truth tellers, there is a need for balance in the areas of love, grace, and truth. We must allow the refining fire of God to challenge our motives, methods, and heart toward others before we speak. Love acts as a protective force against the agenda of hell. Godly love will say extremely difficult things at times, but the motive is pure! This helps to guard our hearts against manipulation and control.

Manipulation is wicked; it moves in the opposite direction of love. A person operating in emotional manipulation tries to be cunning. While the Spirit of God gently leads, demons push and drive. The work of manipulation and emotional witchcraft will put pressure on your mind and emotions in an attempt to control you. It works to override a person's dignity and autonomy with someone else's self-centered wishes or distorted intentions, in a manner that utterly neglects the other individual's worth and honor. This demonic operation demonstrates a clear disdain for the principles of God's Word and His creation. Understanding the tactics and strategies of emotional manipulation will arm you with necessary tools to overcome.

People often default to manipulation out of their own traumas, suffering, or immaturity. This leads them to respond with anxiety and fear instead of engaging in genuine and healthy relationships. They lack the necessary skills required for constructive interactions. They either have never acquired the skills or deliberately avoid developing self-awareness, humility, empathy, and a readiness to accept accountability for their actions. For them, manipulation becomes their primary mode of interaction and the dominant force in their broken relationships.

Humility Versus Pride

There is another class of manipulators who become dependent on others to solve their problems, make excuses on their behalf, or financially support them beyond what's right. This manipulative mindset avoids the normal responsibilities of life and leverages relationships for personal gain. A root heart issue behind manipulation is a lack of humility—being based in pride. Pride is a cunning attribute that sets people up for destruction. It also destroys others through the one who is dominated by its lying mindset.

"When swelling and pride come, then emptiness and shame come also, but with the humble (those who are lowly, who have been pruned or chiseled by trial, and renounce self) are skillful and godly Wisdom and soundness" (Proverbs 11:2 AMPC).

Pride is a gateway to demonic habitation and destruction. The hearts of prideful people are often filled with ungodly ambition. Their goal is self-exaltation, not God-exaltation. This happens in the church world and is often camouflaged as "vision," but it is not godly. God does give vision, and it is often audacious and laborious, but it does not run over other people or create wreckage along the way. Godly vision centers on doing the will of God, loving Jesus, and loving people.

A gifted person who doesn't have a humble heart becomes dangerous. That person's gift can open doors, but their character is not developed. The situation God placed in them to serve others becomes a weapon they use for self-exaltation and destruction. This is one reason I believe prayer is so critical. My late spiritual mother used to say that we need to do a daily "heart check" in prayer. She would encourage me to take my heart before the Lord and ask Him to examine it and purify it. This saved my life many times. There were times that I thought my passion and zeal were for the Lord—but then He would expose a wrong motive or bad attitude, and I would have to go back to prayer. Prayer is a compass! It keeps us pointed in the right direction.

One key to dismantling pride is recognizing Jesus as Lord! When we submit to His authority and majesty, we recognize that we are nothing without Him. This creates dependence on the Lord and breaks the grip of self-reliance.

"And He put all things under His feet, and gave Him to be head over all things to the church, which is His body, the fullness of Him who fills all in all" (Ephesians 1:22–23). It's necessary to realize that Jesus is the head of the church and that all leaders are under-shepherds. No matter how gifted any ministry leader or layperson is, each of us is simply an instrument; He is the conductor. We are called to serve. This revelation will cast down a haughty spirit. Pride puts "me first," and others last. Love is sacrificial, and it serves. Partnering with the love of God and keeping our attitudes in check will dismantle the operation of ungodly pride. It is hard to be prideful when we are genuinely serving others.

Emotional Manipulation's Strategies

If we can define and recognize emotional manipulation and the witchcraft that can accompany it, then we are empowered to break free from it! Let's look at some attributes of a person who may be manipulating you and operating in emotional witchcraft. Identifying the strategies will help you to evaluate and overcome their influence.

Manipulators are seasoned victims. They never take ownership of relationship issues. This is a crafty tool of emotional manipulation, because it places the blame and responsibility on another. This lack of ownership avoids the need for maturity. It also diffuses any necessary confrontation that leads to resolution, because discussion never gets to the real issue. When a manipulative person doesn't get his or her way, the manipulator immediately claims that your lack of compliance is hurting them; they say they are being victimized. They make unrealistic demands and operate in bad character, but then become angry and offended when you refuse to cooperate. The goal here is your surrender! They want you to give in to their desire and demands.

Manipulators are easily offended. When they don't get their way, they get angry. This can manifest through tears, screaming, or pouting. The root issue is that you didn't do what they wanted you to do, so they take offense. Offense is a tricky thing because it creates walls and barriers instead of windows and doors. "A brother offended is harder to win than a strong city, and contentions are like the bars of a castle" (Proverbs 18:19). Once a spirit of offense takes root, it is not looking for a way to forgive or extend mercy; it is looking for a way to prosecute a case! This is one of the wicked aspects of offense. It is a dividing force. Any of us can be offended, but in the case of emotional manipulation and witchcraft, the offense is rooted in desire for control. Truthfully, the "offended" ones are angry because they didn't get their way. The only thing they are looking for from the other party is submission. The issue is this: It is not a form of godly submission. It is demonic domination—pushing, manipulating, and overwhelming.

Manipulators utilize emotional expressions to dominate you. If you confront a person who is using emotional manipulation against you, they may respond in a variety of emotional ways. One common tactic is the silent treatment: They cut you off and avoid you to "punish" you and avoid any form of godly accountability. Another tactic is a dramatic emotional outburst that seems to be out of proportion. This can range from sudden and surprising tears to rage, anger, and yelling. All these manipulations are attempts to put you in defense mode, and thus allow the other person to continue to move ahead with the desired outcome.

Manipulators use accusations against you to gain control. You are talking about one thing, and then suddenly a flurry of accusing arrows is hurled at you. The manipulator calls you names and tells you all the ways that you are wrong. Many times, when this happens in a church context with "prophetic" people, exaggerated spiritual warfare terms are thrown at you. The person who wanted you to volunteer for their event, but you were already committed otherwise, may go from crying to calling you a Jezebel in twenty minutes! You may find yourself shocked with your head swirling. This is what demonic manipulation and control does. It seeks to knock you back on your heels with its force to break past your own will and confuse you. The aim is to ultimately rob you of your God-given freedom!

Manipulators have an unhealthy need for affirmation from others, and so create toxic alignments. Those operating in emotional witchcraft are often reacting to their past pain and so are trying to feel safe and protected. All of us need healthy affirmation, but they have an unhealthy need for affirmation that can become dangerous. When we seek to plug our emotional holes with affirmation, we run the risk of forming alignments with people whom God did not bring to us for His connected purposes. I call these toxic alignments.

Lessons from a Toxic Alignment

I remember a very gifted young woman I mentored years ago. When I first met her, I was struck by her passion for ministry and all the work that she was doing. She never sat still, and was always doing something new and exciting. She went from ministry assignment to ministry assignment. While everything looked great on the outside, darkness was lurking just beneath the surface. Through the years, she had had many different ministry alignments and leaders, but each of them ended in a mess. When you talked to her, she had convincing stories about her stack of broken and troubled relationships. To hear her tell it, she had just had the worst time finding the right people and somehow always seemed to get duped by leaders and accountability partners.

As I entered a relationship with her, I was determined to love her and help her grow. My wife and I, along with our team, poured tons of time and resources into her and her ministry. We wanted to see her win! She quickly tried to engraft herself in much of what I was doing, asking how she could serve and support. She also asked me to help her with projects and vision, and I did so gladly. But over time, I noticed some highly troubling trends. She always had to be the center of attention. When she hosted a guest speaker, she would often take over a service and do a whole lot of ministry before or after the speaker spoke. She had a need to be seen, known, and recognized at all costs. She would leapfrog over people and mishandle relationships to gain prominence. What first looked like honorable diligence was revealed as a toxic quest for prominence and recognition.

The root issue stemmed from a broken and troubled childhood marked by addiction and abandonment. Soon, I began to experience trouble of my own as she sowed seeds of discord in some key relationships in my life. All the tactics I listed above were experienced during that time—the accusations, tears, outbursts, lies, and deception. Eventually, our ministry relationship ended, but not without her creating some collateral damage.

This experience taught me a whole host of lessons. First, I had disregarded a check I'd had in my spirit, overridden by human compassion. Believe your discernment the first time. Your spirit does not lie! Second, both my wife and a dear friend warned me about this person; but again, I didn't listen. I also realized that I had allowed this person too great a role in my life and ministry far too quickly, and I did not establish proper boundaries. I was lured by false promises and empty words. This young minister also came right out of the gate in hot pursuit of relationship. She made all kinds of promises and started calling me her leader long before it was appropriate.

This is another characteristic of a manipulator: The person comes in hot, right out of the gate. As a friend, the person wants you to be his or her BFF and take vacations together. The person desires proximity to you that is too much, too fast. In ministry, the person calls you a spiritual parent, pledges loyalty, and vows to serve your vision, right out of the gate. If this were a romantic situation, this is someone who "love bombs" you! The manipulator wants your attention, your affirmation, and perhaps your resources. The issue is brokenness—the person is trying to feel accepted, powerful, seen, and known. So when things don't go the manipulator's way, that person will defame and accuse you with the same passion with which they once praised you! They create difficult and painful situations when they exit.

Recognizing the Warning Signs

The question to ask ourselves now becomes, *What will help me recognize the signs of emotional manipulation, domination, and witchcraft in my relationships?* Let's begin with this understanding: Healthy relationships produce healthy fruit. Unhealthy relationships produce unhealthy fruit. "He who walks with wise men will be wise, but a companion of fools will be destroyed" (Proverbs 13:20).

Your circle is essential, and it matters to whom you give your ear; those people will have great impact upon you. This is the reason it's imperative to check up on the fruit of anyone you invite into your life. Along with prayer and discernment, this should be top priority.

Second, take time to evaluate the strength and health of your relationships. This is vital. One mistake we humans make in relationships is that we tend to put them on autopilot. This is not wise. We need to examine the positive and negative impact of relationships and be wise in our evaluation and stewardship. As we examine, warning signs become clear indicators that we are being manipulated and falling prey to emotional witchcraft. The following are big, flashing warning signs that you can use to do a quick evaluation:

Your interactions with manipulators consistently leave you feeling drained and exhausted. While godly relationships will require work, they should be life-giving. Unhealthy and controlling relationships zap your emotional, spiritual, and even physical energy. It is never an easy flow, but a burdensome task. In the beginning, it may not feel that way. Often, these toxic entanglements begin with an emotional or spiritual high. It is exciting and may seem like an answer to prayer, but over time the relationship begins to unravel. In the beginning, a skilled manipulator will speak to your desires, your need for affirmation, and possibly your unhealed wounds. This is how they gain access. They are looking to attach, and they are skilled at reading other people and being able to recognize the best avenues to gain access. Eventually, they get comfortable and begin to reveal their true selves. This is when exhausting behaviors unfold. You leave a conversation or interaction depleted. You begin to recognize that these draining behaviors are now a constant reality.

> Living as becomes you] with complete lowliness of mind (humility) and meekness (unselfishness, gentleness, mildness), with patience, bearing with one another and making allowances because you love one another. Be eager and strive earnestly to guard and keep the harmony and oneness of [and produced by] the Spirit in the binding power of peace.
>
> Ephesians 4:2–4 AMPC

You may be trying to stick it out or taking the blame in an unhealthy relationship! A healthy relationship sharpens and enhances *both* people. It is not a one-way street, but a mutual exchange.

You feel as though you are in defensive mode all the time with manipulators. Manipulators often try to make you feel as if you are not allowed to have a different perspective or opinion from theirs. I am not talking about rebellion against authority or being a troublemaker, but about balancing perspectives and having disagreements. When you are battling with being controlled by another person, they become skilled at the art of the redirect. One way they achieve this is by attempting to cause you to feel as though you are wrong for speaking up or stating your opinion. In these cases, the other party typically becomes agitated whenever you voice a different opinion or perspective. That agitation can devolve into a whole range of responses. When emotional witchcraft is involved, you may find your mind swirling in confusion. Prior to the confrontation, you were clear and knew what the issue was, but suddenly, you are feeling lost and unsure. This is the work of evil control, bringing confusion to your mind and working to keep you bound.

Your needs are overlooked and disregarded by manipulators. Healthy relationships require mutual and healthy respect. This first is understanding; you have to seek to understand someone. This shows love and commitment. For example, an introvert may be turned off by the needs of the extrovert to always be out among people. It can become draining and feel very annoying to the introvert, but in reality it is an emotional need for the extrovert. When you seek to understand that other person, you then become aware of and sensitive to his or her needs. One of the gifts of healthy relationships is the beauty of difference! God connects us to other people who see, feel, and process differently than we do. This is not a burden, but a gift. It gives us the opportunity to experience things that we may never have experienced without the presence of that person. It creates a platform for emotional and even spiritual growth. A blatant disregard for the needs of another is essentially a renunciation of that person's value. This is not the norm in a healthy relationship, but it is a hallmark of a manipulative personality.

You are put down by manipulators continually. This leaves you feeling stripped of dignity. It is an immediate confirmation of toxicity. Instead of building up and adding value, the relationship tears down without grace and redemption.

> Let your speech at all times be gracious (pleasant and winsome), seasoned [as it were] with salt, [so that you may never be at a loss] to know how you ought to answer anyone [who puts a question to you].
>
> Colossians 4:6 AMPC

Our words are powerful. The realm of the spirit is voice-activated. Jesus taught us to speak to mountains. When God created the known world in Genesis, He spoke it into existence. There is creative ability in our mouths. What environments and atmospheres do we create in the lives of other people? Are we building up or tearing down? Constant tearing down from another endangers your soul. The words penetrate your heart. You were not created to be cursed on a regular basis. While correction is healthy and relational disagreements are normal, continual nastiness is toxic.

Your feelings are never validated by manipulators. It is important to note that controlling people are self-absorbed. They are extremely insensitive to the thoughts, ideas, and feelings of the people around them. This dangerous pattern of insensitivity and disregard must be noted. If your feelings are repeatedly invalidated, you may find your heart sinking into anger, frustration, or despair.

Your relationship with a manipulator seems extremely one-sided and imbalanced. God ordained relationships to strengthen and enhance you. This doesn't mean that healthy relationships won't have their own challenges. Of course, they will! We are talking about a human connection here, and we are complex people. In a healthy context, there is an equal exchange. It is not one-sided. When a manipulative person enters your life, he or she comes to make continual emotional "withdrawals" without ever making a "deposit." This will lead to emotional exhaustion and frustration. This one-sided mindset may bleed into multiple areas of the relationship. It could be in seeking constant favors from you without ever reciprocating. It may be asking for financial assistance again and again without regard for your needs. It may be in calling you all the time but never genuinely inquiring about your status, only dumping personal frustrations and issues on you. Remember to respect your own value. Your ears are not trash cans!

Heed the Warning Signs

Do you see any of these warning signs in your relationships? Have you found yourself stuck in emotional or spiritual burnout tied to a friendship or other personal relationships? Have you spoken up only to be disregarded or shut down? Is guilt binding you in something that is clearly dysfunctional? After learning about the various manipulative strategies I have listed in this chapter, do you see relationships in your life that are marked by one or more of the warning signs I also listed? If so, you must understand that you are going to have to take action. If you fail to heed the warning signs and make a change, you will fail to progress. The enemy wants to keep you bogged down, angry, and confused.

Here is a disclaimer: I am not vilifying our emotions! Emotions are a wonderful part of our humanity, even when they are messy. The problem with manipulators is their over-the-top emotions they use as a smoke screen to cover up the work of evil control. All relationships will have their ups and downs. They will have times of emotional upheaval and crisis, but in manipulation there is a continual drive to dominate, and these emotional outbursts are tools of evil practices and intent.

All relationships require a measure of grace. God is faithful to lead us to the right people and to bring the right people into our lives. It is a work of grace. We need to pray and believe God for glorious and divine connections. We need to be good stewards over the relationships in our lives. We also need to be wise to discern and properly handle unhealthy relationships that are in our lives, lest they become anchors tying us down instead of releasing us to destiny.

LET'S REFLECT

1. List a few factors that distinguish love from manipulation.
2. Which manipulation or emotional witchcraft strategy have you witnessed in your life? What effect did it have on you?
3. Of all the warning signs listed in this chapter, which one resonates with you the most? When was the last time you received this warning? What will you do about it?

CHAPTER FIVE

Types of Manipulators

"Above all else, guard your heart, for everything you do flows from it" (Proverbs 4:23 NIV). The warning in this verse is that we are to keep and to guard our hearts in the purity of God. The term *guard* suggests the need for vigilance and a proactive mindset. It implies that our hearts can be vulnerable and in need of protection from harmful influences. "For everything you do flows from it." This verse demonstrates the heart's central role in influencing actions and behaviors. It is the source from which moral conduct, critical decisions, and life's activities emanate. When the heart is not in the right place, the pathway becomes polluted.

According to *Strong's Concordance*, the Hebrew word for *heart* in this verse is *leb*.[1] In biblical usage, the heart encompasses much more than the physical organ that pumps our blood through our bodies. It represents the inner person, including the following:

1. *The Mind, thoughts, and seat of decisions:* The heart represents the deepest part of our soul. It is the seat

of reasoning and thinking. Proverbs 23:7 says, "For as he thinks in his heart, so is he." It is the part of us where audacious dreams are stored, decisions are made, and plans are formed.

2. *Emotions and feelings:* The heart is the center of our emotional activity. It houses our feelings, which are a deep and meaningful part of our human journey. Our hearts reflect joy, sorrow, pain, happiness, anger, and love. Psalm 4:7 speaks of joy in the heart, while Proverbs 15:13 mentions a joyful heart making a cheerful face.

3. *Will and decisions:* The heart guides our steps because it is the place where decisions are made. It is where intentions are set, purposes are resolved, and conclusions are drawn. Proverbs 16:9 says, "A man's heart plans his way, but the LORD directs his steps."

4. *Moral center:* The heart represents the core of our moral being. It is the place where convictions are held that align with our belief systems. In fact, it houses the mindsets that comprise the belief systems. It is crucial in discerning right from wrong. Proverbs 18:15 notes, "The heart of the prudent acquires knowledge, and the ear of the wise seeks knowledge."

It's important that we guard our minds, as well. Our mindsets will affect every facet of our lives. We often overlook the instructions of the Lord in Romans 12:2, "Be transformed by the renewing of your mind." Too many believers mistakenly think that because they have been born again, their minds will automatically follow. This sets them up for spiritual and moral failure. The mind is an intricate part of our being that houses beliefs, convictions, memories, worldviews, life goals, trauma, and belief systems. If the critical role of the mind is not fully recognized in our human experience, we will struggle with cycles of failure and pain because we have unrenewed and unhealed areas of our minds.

Facing the Truth, Confronting the Lies

A lot of believers make the mistake of just believing everything will all work out because they love the Lord. This type of Pollyanna approach to Christianity can become reckless and woefully misguided. By ignoring the condition of our own minds, we empower the enemy to lurk in the dark recesses of our unresolved pain and conflict. We stay stuck in mindsets that are far beneath the promises and the majesty of God's glory in our lives. I think some people simply refuse to face the truth because they are afraid to confront the brokenness that exists in their own minds. But when they conceal that brokenness, they empower the work of the enemy in their lives and neglect their own healing and emotional development. We must confront false mindsets and wrong thinking, and then open our souls wide to the healing power of God and all His wonder and majesty.

 The state of our minds is of vital importance to us because our mindsets frame the way we see and react to the world around us. For example, I know believers who think that every adversity is a mark of spiritual warfare in their lives, when that simply is not true. Don't get me wrong, I believe in the invisible realm and the demonic that operates against the destiny of God over our lives. I believe we must fight the good fight of faith with great zeal and power! Yet I also understand that my mind can trap me in a prison from which Jesus already paid the price to set me free. I can blame my current delays and challenges on warfare, but it's wise to check myself and see if it is the result of my own mindset.

I vividly remember that when God started to promote me into different spaces and places, one of the first things I had to deal with was the impostor syndrome. In case you are unfamiliar with the term, it's an inward belief system that says you are not worthy of the places of promotion God brings you to. If we want to connect this in a spiritual sense, we could call it a manifestation of the orphan spirit!

I would be in green rooms with great preachers and leaders, but this thought would arise from the recesses of my mind, *I don't belong here*. This would cause me to withdraw from the tables to which God was inviting me! I had to not only recognize this lie but also confront it with some uncomfortable actions. I began to do spiritual warfare and to pray over my mind and command every devil that was trying to grip my mind to go, in the name of Jesus. I also had to command my flesh to align with the reality of God's promises for my life. So when I would have these feelings, I would do the exact opposite of what they were trying to cause in me. I embraced deliverance in my thinking, which empowered me to rise to another level of destiny and function!

What belief systems are you harboring that contradict the promise of God for your life? What lies might be lurking in the recesses of your mind that need to be uncovered so that God's truth can invade those encampments of the enemy? By being honest and transparent with yourself, you empower the operation of the promises of God in your life. Once you begin to think differently, you will see differently, speak differently, and therefore you will live differently!

Changing the Way We Think

Emotional manipulation and witchcraft find a root system in a troubled mind. A controlling person is typically someone with unresolved trauma who has formed a toxic mindset and uses tools he or she has acquired to manipulate and control the people in their circle. Don't get me wrong, there are spirits involved here, too! Demons have mindsets. When a demon dwells in the life of a person, it afflicts them with a false belief system that attempts to take over their personality. The goal of the spirit is to act out its wicked desires through the person.

> So all the demons begged Him, saying, "Send us to the swine, that we may enter them." And at once Jesus gave them permission. Then the unclean spirits went out and entered the swine (there were about two thousand); and the herd ran violently down the steep place into the sea, and drowned in the sea.
>
> Mark 5:12–13

Jesus cast the legion of demons out of the region of the Gadarenes. This man who contained them was their house. They were now just spirits without bodies. They sought out bodies to live in and Jesus gave them permission to enter the swine. The swine reacted by committing suicide. When a person receives deliverance and the spirit is cast out, however, the mindset doesn't automatically change. There must be a process of girding up the loins of the mind and changing the way we think. We must confront error with truth. This is the reason the Word of God is such a critical tool in every person's deliverance journey.

The Word of God will point us in the right direction when an unhealed mind is trying to deceive us. Many times, people operating in emotional witchcraft will justify their behaviors because of past trauma and false belief systems. When whole people come into their lives and refuse to submit to their manipulation, they become angry and often attack them. They will accuse them of having a wrong spirit. This deception has lodged in their minds. This is the reason broken people feel better around other broken people. There is no challenge to their mindsets or behaviors. They feel accepted, because there is a shared toxicity.

People who have a different mindset point out the dysfunctional behavior, and it brings a reaction of pain and anger from the manipulator. The truth is, deliverance can take time and it will not always feel good! When we are unlearning old patterns, it may be tough. When we are renouncing evil vows, it can be hard work. When we are breaking soul ties, we may feel all kinds of emotions.

We need to be like the woman with the issue of blood in Mark 5 and press in, no matter what. She had received a death diagnosis, but faith arose inside her. She determined that she was going to get up and get to Jesus, no matter what. Her faith overrode her pain and the words of the doctors. That is how faith works. Faith makes a way when there seems to be no way. Part of breaking the cords of emotional manipulation and witchcraft is learning to identify and break free from people who would attempt to control you. This is exceedingly important, because emotional manipulation is a kind of witchcraft that will contaminate your mind, cause you pain and anger, and even greatly hinder or shipwreck your destiny. God planned every facet of your life with great attention to detail—don't let the enemy derail your progress!

Eleven Specific Manipulators

The enemy wants to hinder and abort your purpose by pushing you in the wrong direction and wasting your time and energy. This is what the presence of a manipulator will do. Let's look at eleven specific types of manipulators whom I find to be at the forefront of emotional witchcraft.

1. *The bold boss.* The bold boss always needs to be in charge, catered to, and often lacks empathy toward others. In a family, this is the person who refuses to participate unless they were the one who made the plans. If you set the barbecue time at 5 p.m., this person will insist on changing it to 6 p.m. They don't play on a court you choose because they need to feel in control. This person is also a bully whose primary power is force. They force people to bend to their ways. In the workplace, they operate in heavy levels of control, making unreasonable demands and having very little tolerance for the opinions or ideas of others. Their main mode of control is through making demands! They have extremely demanding personalities with a need to feel in charge. When they don't gain your submission, you quickly become the enemy.

2. *The overbearing rescuer.* This person leverages acts of kindness into a debt that must be repaid by obeying them

and catering to them. They hold anything they do for you over your head as a tool of manipulation. These people enter your life loaded with helpful suggestions, gifts, and services. It may feel like they are an answer to prayer, but there is an unseen motive—to gain control in your life. They don't enter loud and bold, they enter appearing kind and meek. They need to feel powerful, and accomplish this by dominating others and entangling them in their affairs. This is the overbearing family member who will provide money but then want to micromanage you. This is the minister of helps who offers so much to the preacher, but the real goal is to gain access to the power the person sees on that preacher. This is the assistant who wants to be the sole gatekeeper of the boss. This type of person takes on the lives of other people as a project. They can be hard to spot, because their approach starts with apparent kindness.

3. *The outspoken victim.* There is a lot of power in appearing powerless. Many people use the "poor me" narrative to achieve their objectives and continually get their way. They reel people into their cause by sharing all their past tragedies. They refuse to take inventory of their lives with any form of sober accountability; instead, they love to highlight the failures of others. They are big talkers! They have a million and one stories and are skilled in turning people against one another. They curse their friends, call them Jezebels, and then tell others how they were victimized, even when they were the aggressors. This type of manipulator thrives on drama, and accusation is the choice weapon. They are masterful at "selling their narrative." They have loads of experience. They have been through lots of relationships, many churches, and have switched jobs frequently. They never have

a good testimony of past relationships. When they exit a relationship, they do it loudly and with no godly order. In fact, they love dramatic exits. They post about it, talk about it, and slash and burn on their way out. They lack healthy communication and resolution skills.

4. *The influencer.* The influencer thrives on shared offense. They feel upset, but being insecure, don't want to be alone. They create a team of allies. There is a web around them that entangles other people in damaging conflicts. They look to influence your thoughts with a subtle type of witchcraft in which they personalize a problem that is not your problem. They may share this in the vein of a warning and concern, but the root behind it is strife, division, and offense. They operate in carnal and demonic wisdom void of maturity and the love of God. They vilify those who do not submit to their opinions or aren't offended by what they're offended by. If you don't agree with them or entertain their point of view, they are not at peace. As with all forms of demonic bondage, they are driven and lack peace. They may even be deceived to believe that they are fighting a righteous war, and that all the collateral damage is because of other people. Yet the common denominator in all the strife is them.

5. *The prophet (you didn't know you needed).* This prophetic type of manipulator brings spiritual revelation to you without regard for your personhood, preferences, or boundaries. They use their prophetic revelation as a form of unsanctified bullying. Here is the thing: A true prophet knows when to speak and when to pray. He or she has no interest in dominating others. But a manipulator or witch seeks to dominate and control others! This type of controlling person plays on the other person's desire to be right with

God. They love to give partial warnings like, "Something is just off. You'd better pray." They plant the seed, and then let you imagine what they may be saying. The goal is to get you aligned with them and dependent upon their revelation. Bolder types of prophetic deceivers may just blurt out their whole accusation. If you do a fruit inspection, you will find a few things. First, you will find a track record of rebellion and a lack of submission. You will find that they have made messes in any ministry they have been part of. You will also find that they lack the love of God toward others. They are loud and proud! They refuse to consider the well-being of others, choosing instead to prosecute their own case against another. They do not understand or embrace godly reconciliation. They rail against the grace of God and despise others, but hide their anger under spiritual language. It goes far beyond sharing; they throw their insights at you and warn you of impending doom if you do not agree with their opinions and thoughts. They believe that they are the voice of God in your life and have a polluted prophetic perspective. Think Jezebel! That is their behavioral pattern. When you don't submit to their revelation, they will curse you. You need to continually use the blood and the name of Jesus as weapons against such control and accusation. Praying and breaking every lie that is hurled against you is a vital tool.

6. *The overly concerned communicator.* These manipulators let you know that they are only guiding you because they love you. They take no account of the pressure or the confusion they are causing; instead, they forge ahead and are determined to let you know that all they are doing is for your own good. They overstep their place in your life and breeze past normal relational boundaries to tell you what

they think about your decisions and friends. You may have a casual relationship, but they storm the gates as if they are your most trusted advisers. When you attempt to stop their aggression, they will feel hurt and will let you know about it! They will remind you of the "care" they have expressed toward you and how they thought you felt the same way. Remember, all of this was uninvited! You never asked these people to rush into your personal affairs with their thoughts and opinions; they do this on their own. It gives them a false sense of purpose and meaning.

7. *The messy micromanager.* This is a highly organized and motivated manipulator who feels the need to force you to move according to their timelines and preferences. When they get involved in your life, they try to take over details they should not be involved in. They desire to be in charge and to force a submission on your part. They typically operate in a lot of anxiety because they throw themselves into the lives of others who are making plans. They are big on things going their way! You cannot engage them with any sense of independence. They need to control each facet of an interaction to feel secure. They love to provide "guidance" to others, and get angry when it is refused. If you are planning a meet-up and don't heed their suggestions, they will immediately display a poor attitude or will withdraw. They view people as projects and find a sense of purpose in entangling themselves in the lives of others in an unhealthy way. There is healthy help that empowers others, and then there is unhealthy help that dominates others. They engage in the latter.

8. *The rogue leader.* This person flourishes particularly well in church circles. He or she is confident about what

everyone else must do, yet the person has a long track record of broken relationships and an anti-submissive attitude. This person forces others to submit even though this manipulator type shuns submission. This manipulator postures himself or herself as an expert, even though the person's track record is bad. Overconfident and overly opinionated, the primary issue is that the person wants to lead without any desire to be led. This manipulator breaches protocols and disregards any form of order. When another confronts or addresses his or her lack of order, the person retaliates, usually defaulting to spiritual language to curse the other person—with great venom and intense passion. There is a strong need to be seen and to feel important, so this person will gravitate to places and relationships that meet those needs. This person's participation is contingent upon the other party yielding to them and meeting their needs to be seen and known. When those needs are not met, this manipulator will exit.

9. *The disconnected visionary.* This is a manipulative leader who is on a mission and sees you as a tool to achieve his or her vision, but the danger is a lack of regard for your well-being. This can be in business, family, or church. The person will sacrifice you on the altar of their success, with little empathy. This person may be deceived into thinking that he or she is doing the Lord's work. The truth is, the vision may have been granted by God, but their administration of the vision is lacking; there is no capacity to care for others.

These people can be profound leaders and builders, but struggle to maintain wellness among those they lead. They will leverage the strength of the vision to pressure people to go beyond an appropriate level of involvement. Manipulation kicks in when, instead of allowing God to bring the right people and lead them, they begin to operate in the flesh, recruiting and driving the people. They preach a hardcore "work now and rest later" message. They are unmoved by calamity and collateral damage. They want to be successful at all costs and view people only as tools for their vision. When you are no longer useful to them, you will immediately be cut off.

Yet remember—some apostolic visionaries do have a tenacious work ethic and massive dreams! We can read this description and falsely categorize them here. The difference is spiritual and emotional health. Even the most driven leader can be healthy! The healthy leader cares for others and is moved with compassion when there is a crisis. The healthy leader may build in rapid-fire succession, but he or she loves and values the people God brings and doesn't desire to control them. Unhealthy visionaries crave control and unhealthy domination. They use people to get what they can from them, and then discard them when they deem them no longer useful.

10. *The overgrown child.* This type of manipulator is an immature person who has widely unrealistic expectations and has mastered the art of being needy. They do not have a healthy mindset or life skills. They believe that their challenges and issues are the responsibilities of others. They have loads of stories about the hard things that they have faced, but they have done very little to grow. They are skillful at building relationships with those who have deep feelings of guilt. They leverage the sense of guilt to get others to bow to their desires. In appearing disempowered, they skillfully get others to do their bidding. They are masterful at gaining money and help from others. Their manipulative superpower

is appearing weak and needy. But beneath is hidden a deep well of control. They thrive by getting others to manage their problems, handle their responsibilities, and meet their needs. They neglect their own responsibilities; therefore, crisis is their norm! They thrive in environments of upheaval, because they are used to it.

11. The dominating guardian. This is a family member or pseudo family member who trespasses healthy boundaries and pulls on the heartstrings to keep you stuck in a space that is wildly unhealthy and outdated. The person disempowers your growth by making you feel inadequate and does not desire to see you move toward healthy independence, because their presence and domination in your life fulfills their need. This can become extremely damaging to other relationships. When parents act this way toward their grown children, it can become a portal of strife and division in marriages. When you begin to set boundaries with this type of manipulator, they will cry, pout, and express deep hurt. They may also try to convince you that you are unable to make it without them or to do things on your own. They will speak to your insecurities and do their best to make you dependent upon them. They look for relationships where they can have the upper hand through codependence.

Slamming Doors Shut to the Enemy

Now that we have identified some of the various types of manipulators, it is essential to shift our focus from merely identifying these traits to taking actionable steps in dealing with them. Awareness is the first step! Now we must also ask, *What do I do with this knowledge?* We need to focus both on protecting ourselves and continuing to grow in wisdom and discernment.

Of course, we do not want to use these tools as a means of accusation against others! It is easy to find fault and attack. What we want to do is learn and grow so that we are able to slam doors shut to the enemy. It's not just about recognizing these manipulative behaviors but also about developing the right strategies to effectively counteract them. The primary tool we have at our disposal is the Word of God. The Bible offers profound wisdom and guidance on how to navigate difficult relationships and demonic attacks. Let's look at a few specific ways from the Word to slam the doors shut on emotional witchcraft.

Embrace and understand healthy emotional and relationship boundaries. All manipulators cross normal boundaries with little regard for others. We do not set boundaries to punish or to keep others out, but to become the healthiest version of ourselves. Proverbs 25:28 states, "Whoever has no rule over his own spirit is like a city broken down, without walls." This verse emphasizes the importance of self-control and holding the responsibility for your life, decisions, and relationships. Your boundaries should honor your mission and your vision.

Grow in wisdom and discernment over time. Discernment allows us to see beyond the surface and understand the true intentions of others, along with hidden matters of the heart. James 1:5 encourages us, "If any of you lacks wisdom, let him ask of God, who gives to all liberally and without reproach, and it will be given to him." It's vital to continually seek God's wisdom. Wisdom empowers us to live godly and healthy lives.

Be intentional about fostering healthy relationships. This can be challenging and it does take work, but it is also greatly rewarding. Finding people with similar values and vision is life-giving. Healthy relationships are empowering and characterized by mutual respect, honesty, and support. Toxic relationships, on the other hand, drain your energy, demand a lot of you, and often involve manipulative tactics. By fostering healthy relationships, you create a supportive environment that will disempower the lies of the enemy and encourage your growth and resilience. Proverbs 17:17 reminds us that "a friend loves at all times, and a brother is born for adversity."

Pay attention to the warnings! When you meet someone, and there is a check in your spirit, pay attention. Manipulation will try to say one thing to you, even though you see something different. Believe your spirit! This does not mean that God won't send you into the lives of the hurting. Jesus does His best work in the messy spaces. You may be sent to someone that has all kinds of issues, but you are more effective when you first can discern and respond accordingly. Remember that the devil wants to blindside you, but you have the mind of Christ.

The Holy Spirit Has the Answers

Do you see yourself in any of the eleven types of manipulators I covered? What will you do to repent and remove the use of emotional witchcraft from your life?

Do you have any colleagues or friends who match these descriptions? How can you respond to them differently? What appropriate boundaries do you need to set?

Being equipped to recognize the operation of emotional manipulation empowers you to clearly see it. Then, with prayer and wise strategy, you can break its grip. Underneath the bad behaviors of a manipulator is a hurting person. Jesus was moved with compassion when He saw the broken. Recognize that even if you need to exit such people's circles, you can still pray for them.

God will give you wisdom on how to move forward to slam the doors shut on emotional manipulation and witchcraft (which we'll talk about more in the next chapter). He will show you what to do, and the Spirit of the Lord will break all the clutter off your mind. The enemy wants you to feel helpless and overwhelmed, but it's a lie! The Holy Spirit has the answers, and He will guide your pathway forward.

LET'S REFLECT

1. List three beliefs you have held that contradict what God has said about you.
2. Of the list of eleven specific manipulators, which kind do you find yourself encountering the most? Why do you think that is?
3. Now that you are aware of various types of manipulators and their tactics, list three action steps that you can take to address their presence in your life.

CHAPTER SIX

Closing Open Doorways

"Nor give place to the devil" the apostle Paul said in Ephesians 4:27. We can give the devil a place, a legal access in our lives, by opening a door! In my experience, a tough case of deliverance has often come through a door I have had to uncover. What door had been opened? Perhaps it was abuse and trauma from years ago, maybe illicit sexual activity, or possibly unresolved bitterness. Once the doorway is identified, it is time to close that door and cut all demonic attachments. The same is true for shutting down the operation of emotional manipulation and witchcraft. First getting to the bottom of what invited the unhealthy relationship, and then seeing what created an environment for it to thrive, are vital parts of freedom and spiritual growth.

What does a door do? It acts as a means of passage. You can enter or exit a space through a doorway. If you close and lock a door, you have secured that space. I want to help you secure the sacred spaces of your life by identifying and closing any open doors. I have often talked to people who seem to fall prey to manipulation repeatedly—as though they are a magnet for it. It is awful to witness, because they are in pain and frustrated. But manipulation is a form of deception: The enemy focuses them on the activity of the one who is afflicting them, but the reality is that they need to give an account for their own participation. It's important to ask, *What is my responsibility in this situation?*

This may sound tough, but once you own your part and take back your authority, you make quick progress. In our walk with God, it is crucial to understand that we can inadvertently open doors to the enemy, allowing evil influences to infiltrate our lives. These doors are often opened through our minds, our mouths, our belief systems, and unresolved soul wounds. When left unchecked, these openings can tie us to the wrong people, hinder us on our journey, and subject us to domination and emotional manipulation at the hands of others. We find ourselves frustrated and exhausted, seemingly without answers.

Healing from Traumatized Belief Systems

Our minds are the creative engines of our lives, and thus they determine our course. Belief systems that were formed during trauma become lying influences that try to dictate our actions. For instance, we may believe that we are unlovable because a parent left us, and now we keep falling prey to bad relationships, looking for love! We put up with abuse, because deep down inside there is a dominant thought: *This is what I deserve.* Perhaps we wrestle with rejection due to "church hurt," and when we feel as though someone may be getting ready to reject us, we forcefully push them away.

These belief systems become dangerous patterns that contaminate our relationships.

Philippians 4:8 (AMPC) provides invaluable instruction regarding our thought life:

> For the rest, brethren, whatever is true, whatever is worthy of reverence and is honorable and seemly, whatever is just, whatever is pure, whatever is lovely and lovable, whatever is kind and winsome and gracious, if there is any virtue and excellence, if there is anything worthy of praise, think on and weigh and take account of these things [fix your minds on them].

By cutting off cycles of negative thinking, and dwelling on God's Word, we can change our dominant thought patterns. God's Word is truth! It trumps our past experiences. I am not suggesting that we bury the pain. Instead, we experience it, and then subject it to God's Word. His Word is a healing balm for our broken hearts.

Our words have the power to form an environment around us. We need to ask ourselves daily whether we are speaking out of faith or fear. We also need to evaluate agreements we have made with the lies of the enemy, and break them. Dwelling on negativity and speaking in agreement with the enemy regarding our lives will create bonds with pain and trauma. These are spiritual laws! When we first believe, and then speak, we create alignment. This can be an open door for all kinds of spiritual and emotional problems.

James 3:6 warns us about the dangers of the tongue: "And the tongue is a fire, a world of iniquity. The tongue is so set among our members that it defiles the whole body, and sets on fire the course of nature; and it is set on fire by hell." Ephesians 4:29 (AMPC) advises,

> Let no foul or polluting language, nor evil word nor unwholesome or worthless talk [ever] come out of your mouth, but only such [speech] as is good and beneficial to the spiritual progress of others, as is fitting to the need and the occasion, that it may be a blessing and give grace (God's favor) to those who hear it.

By guarding our speech and ensuring that our words build up rather than tear down, we can slam demonic doors shut.

Soul wounds are broken places in our minds that can create openings for the enemy to exploit, leading to further pain and manipulation. These wounds often tie us to people with toxic mindsets who hinder our journey and manipulate our emotions. Psalm 147:3 offers hope for healing: "He heals the brokenhearted and binds up their wounds." Jesus had a profound ministry of healing souls. He took every soul wound to Calvary, so that we could be healed in our minds. Allowing the Lord and His power to come into every facet of our minds is essential. Too often, we hide in shame, but the answer is in His power.

Discerning Open Doors

The first part of Philippians 2:5 encourages us, "Let this mind be in you which was also in Christ Jesus." Jesus would not tell us to do something that was impossible in His power. We can access the mind of Christ by faith and communion (relationship) with Him. We need to get into His Word, engage in prayer, and pursue the things of God. We need to be vulnerable and allow Him into the painful and broken places of our lives. It is one thing to recognize the need to slam demonic doors closed, and it is another thing to dive deeply into methodology to discern open doors. This becomes one of the most imperative components of our journey to freedom and rejecting emotional manipulation and witchcraft.

According to Webster's online dictionary, the word *discernment* means "the quality of being able to grasp and comprehend what is obscure: skill in discerning," and "an act of perceiving or discerning something."[1] Discernment deals with our ability to perceive hidden things. According to 1 Corinthians 12, there is a supernatural gift of the discerning of spirits. This gift bypasses the natural realm and peers into the operation of spiritual influences.

For example, the gift of discerning of spirits will allow us to perceive an unusual presence of the Lord in a corporate gathering. It will also allow us to detect the presence of angels in our midst. The discerning of spirits is also vital to exposing Satan's undercover operations. When our spiritual eyes, ears, and senses are activated and alerted, we can discern the wrong spirit that is hiding in the dark.

In addition to the supernatural gift of the discerning of spirits, we can also operate in levels of discernment through knowledge and maturity. When we become accustomed to the operating mode of certain demonic entities, we can easily track their footprints in the affairs of life. Once we learn the tactics of controlling spirits, it becomes much easier to identify them.

With that in mind, let's discuss some keys to help us discern open doorways in our lives that invite emotional manipulation and witchcraft. Specifically, I want to look at *demonic patterns and cycles*, *prophetic patterns and dreams*, *contemplative prayer*, and *not bearing false burdens*. Using these keys, we are going to become masterful at both detecting the spiritual doors and intentionally closing them. We are also going to become activated in receiving the healing ministry of Jesus, allowing it to saturate our souls and hearts with the power of His Spirit, so that we can walk in total victory.

Demonic Patterns and Cycles

When there is demonic influence in our lives, it will manifest in patterns and cycles. We often notice these as repetitious occurrences in our lives. For example, those who struggle with a vagabond spirit can step back from the current situation and look through the history of their spiritual lives. They can quickly detect instability, and see where they had an unction to relocate and be part of a life-giving ministry, only to fall into boredom or spiritual dissatisfaction that led to a sudden move. Over time, they'll see that there is a lifespan of connectivity with wise and capable leadership that ultimately ends in an abrupt exit. They will see that throughout their continuous journey of instability, they've lost essential traction, financial breakthroughs, and necessary spiritual relationships, due to their own false prophetic leadings. The ability to track and monitor these movements becomes the detection system for demonic influences.

Some time ago, a ministerial network that I knew of faced a stunning collapse. There was a swirl of spiritual warfare around the leader and its participants. Many of the network affiliates pulled out, attacking and accusing the leader of poor moral choices and of stifling, controlling behavior. Observing this from a distance, I could see that one of the core elements was pride in the heart of the leader and opportunism in the hearts of many of the network members. I watched as they began to seek out other affiliations and connections, and I wondered, *Will they learn their lessons, or will they continue down the same pathways, only with a different face?*

I was stunned to watch the answer to my questions unfold. Many of those involved began to be drawn to other leaders who essentially embodied the same characteristics of brokenness, but with a different external presentation. I could see that their own hearts were drawn to toxicity—it was familiar to them. I marveled as I realized that they were in a holding pattern in their emotional and spiritual lives, and about to repeat the same damaging cycle they had just escaped.

I use this example because it bears true in many of our lives. We keep repeating similar patterns and cycles, only to place blame on the other participants in our story. We may connect with people who are overly controlling, only to exit the relationship in anger or frustration at the manipulation and dominance! Yet the very next relationship we connect with holds the exact same measure of impurity.

We first need to pull back to widen our view so we can evaluate our own heart conditions. As we realize that there is something in us that needs to be healed, we can see how it continues to draw us to the same type of people and situations again and again. This cyclical nature of events discloses to us the presence of an open door. Where was the door opened? Perhaps it was opened through a tumultuous childhood. Maybe it was opened through a difficult divorce. On the other hand, there may be an internal battle for acceptance that draws us to people with strong personalities. The answer is not in vilifying the people who have been part of our journey, not even those who were demonized. The answer is in recognizing the doorway! When we get to the root of the problem, seek out healing and deliverance, we can then slam that door closed for good!

Pause here and take an inventory of your life and relationships. Do you see a reoccurrence of certain troubling behaviors and cycles in your life? Is there an ongoing battle in your relationships? As I said earlier, relationships involve our humanity and therefore can be messy. Don't condemn or beat yourself up because you are human and have engaged other humans in the normal ebb and flow of life and relationships. This is all part of the journey that is before you. But it is important for you to observe any patterns or cycles that point you toward any level of bondage and the need for healing.

Prophetic Patterns and Dreams

Now, I also want you to observe prophetic patterns in your life. It has always been my conviction that when God has an important message for us, He will repeat it a number of times! So often, our own "orphan mentality" creates a platform of fear in our hearts. We think we're going to miss God's message for us, as if it is a fleeting glimpse of the possibility. We easily forget that He is a good Father who will make the message resoundingly clear in our hearts.

> For God may speak in one way, or in another, yet man does not perceive it. In a dream, in a vision of the night, when deep sleep falls upon men, while slumbering on their beds, then He opens the ears of men, and seals their instruction.
>
> Job 33:14–16

This is one of my favorite passages regarding prophetic dreams. God is always faithful to communicate to us what is necessary for our lives and journey. One of the ways that He speaks to us is in the night season. We will examine more about that later, but I want to extrapolate from these verses the principle that the Lord will speak to us in multiple ways and times to get His message across.

When you look at this process in your life, I call it the "examination of prophetic history." What has God already said about you and your destiny? What has God said multiple times? That is a prophetic pattern and a key indicator for your destiny, and it gives you the answer to slamming doors shut to spiritual and emotional evil!

> And the LORD called Samuel again the third time. So he arose and went to Eli, and said, "Here I am, for you did call me." Then Eli perceived that the LORD had called the boy. Therefore Eli said to Samuel, "Go, lie down; and it shall be, if he calls you, that you must say, 'Speak, LORD, for your servant hears.'" So Samuel went and lay down in his place. Now the LORD came and stood and called as at other times,

"Samuel! Samuel!" And Samuel answered, "Speak, for your servant hears."

1 Samuel 3:8–10

The Lord was speaking to the child Samuel in this passage. His audible voice was beckoning for the attention of the young seer. He didn't stop speaking after the first time; He kept on speaking. This provides a prophetic template for us to follow in our lives. When God is trying to deliver us from a doorway, He will speak to us repeatedly about the solution to the problem. Many times, we just aren't paying attention. In fact, sometimes we fail to interpret His message because we don't realize the prophetic symbolism. All throughout the Word of God, His voice spoke in a plethora of ways. God can speak through hearing; speak through vision and sight; through the senses of taste, touch, and smell; and through symbols and dream language. The failure to pay attention to or improperly interpret the voice of God is what causes the message to be missed.

Many times, when God is trying to reveal to you what exists in the unseen realm, He'll do it through prophetic dreams. The question becomes, *Why would God speak to me in a dream and not just speak to me while I'm awake?* The answer is both complex and simple, but let's consider one possibility: God may be speaking to you in the night because your conscious mind is suspended and your emotional attachments are irrelevant.

For example, when I was a young church planter excited about the expanding ministry God had given to me in a rural area of America, it often felt like my back was against the wall, despite the great breakthrough we were experiencing.

I faced unrelenting cycles of spiritual and emotional warfare. I was struggling to find the answers that would explain the viciousness of attack that the ministry and I continued to experience. One night I went to sleep, not thinking about any of those circumstances, and had a stunning prophetic dream. The dream was not straightforward, but a portion of the dream dealt with people not paying attention while I was talking. There was an old figure in the dream who was whispering in the ears of people and sowing discord. There were so many different layers of this dream that I had to write it all down, then look through it and pray over it.

As I began to unravel the contents of the dream, it became clear to me that the Lord was showing me a religious spirit that was sowing seeds of strife in the congregants and whispering accusations throughout the people of God. I began to pray after the dream was interpreted for God to reveal a strategy to break the grip of these foul spirits. The dream became a platform for strategic operations to overcome the enemy. Had I not understood dream language, I would have simply chalked it up to an unusual dream that didn't make any sense. But I realized that when God speaks in prophetic dreams, He often does so through symbols.

"I will bless the LORD who has given me counsel; my heart also instructs me in the night seasons" (Psalm 16:7). Here are three common elements of recognizing a prophetic dream:

1. *There is a sense of urgency.* You wake up with a deep impression of the significance of the dream. You can't seem to shake it, even though you may not understand it.

2. *There is a sense of either God's peace, wisdom, or warning.* Prophetic dreams contain a message.
3. *It may come as a big surprise, because it may be something you didn't know or see before.* This is one of the elements of prophetic dreams, but prophecy will be layered, and directional messages will come to you several times in several ways.

A person can never interpret a dream that he or she does not record! I always encourage people to keep either a device with digital recording capabilities or a journal on their nightstand. When they wake from a dream that feels as though it was in high definition and has a sense of urgency, they need to write or record the dream immediately. This empowers the person to be able to go back and pray over and interpret the dream.

Examine the symbolism in your dream. Most prophetic dreams are in the language of symbolism. If you examine prophetic dreams from the Bible, they often required an interpretation because God spoke through pictures and symbols. So the first thing to ask is, *Are any of these symbols in my dream also in the Bible? Do these symbols hold personal meaning in my life?* Then begin to break down the potential meanings of the symbols in the dream, while you are praying for understanding and listening to the Lord. If God sent the dream, He knows what He wants to show you!

A prophetic dream that is not interpreted becomes a message that is not received! Understanding and discerning prophetic dreams is not natural, but supernatural. Being a student of dream language will help you acquire the necessary skills to be able to properly pray over and interpret your dream. God took the time to visit you in your dream life because He wanted to show you something: It may be an avenue of escape, an area that needs deliverance, a critical warning, or instructions for your next season. Ask Him what you need to know, and ask Him often.

Contemplative Prayer

Another tool in discerning and closing any open doors that the enemy has established is *contemplative prayer*. "Be still, and know that I am God; I will be exalted among the nations, I will be exalted in the earth" (Psalm 46:10). You may ask, "What is contemplative prayer?" I want to give you three facets of it. First, contemplative prayer is a form of prayer in which you sit in silence and stillness, focusing your heart and mind on the presence of God. This allows the canvas of your mind to be illuminated by the greatest artist in history, Yahweh.

"I will meditate on Your precepts and have respect to Your ways [the paths of life marked out by Your law]. I will delight myself in Your statutes; I will not forget Your word" (Psalm 119:15–16 AMPC).

A second element of contemplative prayer is meditation on Scripture. When we think about meditating on the Word of God, we're literally thinking about digesting a certain Scripture, not simply reading it. It's a combination of reading, writing, speaking it aloud, and pondering its deeper meaning. It is allowing the Scripture to move from being only information in your mind into faith within your spirit.

Third, contemplative prayer is a time of intentional listening. Never has this been more needed than in today's world filled with distraction and the constant hum of life and activity. When God was dealing with Elijah, He revealed the necessity of tuning in to the still, small voice. I fear that many of us overlook critical instructions because we don't practice stillness. We may know how to decree and declare, how to bind and loose, but we don't know how to sit and be still. It's in the places of stillness that God's voice resounds deep within us to provide the insight that will preserve and protect us. It's in the places of stillness that we hear the thing that has been overlooked, the missing ingredient and the key to our next level of faith. It's in the places of stillness that the ending of a season is released into our spirit and the entryway to the next assignment is revealed to us.

The prophetic is composed of awareness at its highest level and potential. But if we fail to become still, we fail to become aware. Therefore, you and I cannot afford to live our lives busy and tuned out to the still, small voice of God. If you're going to make room for God in your life so you can slam doors shut and receive deliverance and emotional healing, you must practice the art of stillness. The voice of God is always speaking, but the question for each of us becomes, *Am I listening?*

Contemplative prayer becomes a platform through which you listen to God and tune out the world around you. You may be only one seeking session away from the answer you need to slam demonic doors shut. We need to know how to pray effectively and posture our hearts to discover and then close any doors that have empowered emotional manipulation and witchcraft in our lives. Begin by praying over your heart, which is composed of your mind, soul, and will. Speak aloud Scriptures that describe the presence of peace in your mind and the validity of having the mind of Christ.

When the Spirit of the Lord began to deal with me about Jesus as the healer of our souls, He told me to begin to preach Scriptures like Luke 4:18, in which Jesus declares that He restores our soul. I asked the Lord, *What am I to do after I've taught and preached on this? How will you demonstrate it?*

The Lord said simply, *Lead people to me as their healer.*

If you study the Scriptures, Jesus was known for His amazing healing ministry, but it was not limited to physical ailments alone; it also reached to the depth of brokenness in the human mind. As I would preach on Jesus the soul healer, and then call people to the altar, He would meet them there. He began to reveal to me that when we call upon His presence, He will respond. So I want to encourage you to begin to pray daily over your soul. Find some Scriptures that minister to you and speak to you about the potential for a healed mind and decision maker. When your decision maker is not consecrated, your pathway is polluted. You must be intentional about praying over your mind, aligning yourself with the Word of God, and inviting the healing presence of Jesus into the deep recesses of your emotions.

Not Bearing False Burdens

We must also ask ourselves the question, *Am I bearing false burdens?* One thing that will empower emotional manipulation from others is taking responsibility for people and situations that simply do not belong to you. For example, because of past trauma and rejection, you may feel it is your duty to say yes to every request that is made of you—but then you live your life burdened, overwhelmed, and frustrated. You pray prayers of deliverance from exhaustion, but your yes to bearing false burdens is causing you to keep a door open to exhaustion in your life.

What false burdens are you bearing today? Do you have a problem saying no to things you are not responsible for? You may need to learn the art of a sanctified no! For every yes in your life, there will have to be a no. For instance, if I say yes to traveling to another nation, I'm going to have to say no to some requests from people who want to meet with me in the United States. They may become hurt and loudly express their frustration with me. But I resolve in my heart that I am where I need to be, doing what God told me to do. When we obey God, we leave the consequences to Him.

Remember how Jesus did not leave to address His friend Lazarus's sickness immediately? In the time that passed between the request and His departure to minister to Lazarus, his dear friend died. All hope seemed lost, but what people did not realize is that God is never late; He is always on time! Jesus raised Lazarus from the dead and turned a mess into a miracle. Submitting to God's intention and timing positions you to partner with the supernatural in your life.

Another part of not opening the door to bearing false burdens is to ask, *Do I attract emotionally unhealthy people? If so, why?* Use any repeated relational failures as a mirror to examine your own heart. Where is there a need in you for emotional healing, counseling, and deliverance? Ask yourself, *Am I continually drawn to toxic people? If so, what is it in me that needs to change?*

It is not your responsibility to change anyone else. You have no control over how somebody else responds or reacts to your needs or requests. When there's a crisis in a relationship, the only thing you can do is govern your own heart attitude. Stop taking responsibility for what is not your responsibility, and then you can begin to focus on your own health and development. This will close demonic doorways that ought to never be open, and open divine doorways that had seemed closed to you before.

○○○○○○○○○○○○ LET'S REFLECT ○○○○○○○○○○○○

1. In what ways are you creating open doorways to the enemy with the things you (or others in your life) are saying or have said repeatedly?
2. Document some ways that you have believed or agreed with the enemy in those words. Then document what God says concerning that thought and those words.
3. Do this often. Seek to make this part of the process of guarding your speech.

CHAPTER SEVEN

Breaking Soul Ties and Evil Alliances

I once had a startling encounter with a wife whom I was counseling. She had been previously married, stuck in a very contentious relationship with turbulent ups and downs. However, she was now remarried to a man who loved the Lord and was faithful and diligent. Though from the outside it appeared she now had a good marriage, there was some internal unrest. As I spoke with the couple, the root problem became clear: Even though her previous relationship had been extremely unhealthy and riddled with abuse, there was still a craving for her former partner. She was bound to him in an invisible sense, even though she despised his vile contributions to her life.

What could this be? I asked myself. Immediately, I knew I was dealing with a soul tie. A soul tie is the knitting of two souls (emotions, minds, and hearts) together. When two people get married and consummate their union, an automatic soul tie is formed.

In marriage, this is not an ungodly soul tie, but a godly one! "For this reason a man shall leave his father and mother and be joined to his wife, and the two shall become one flesh" (Ephesians 5:31). Within the context of marriage and its sexual intimacy, there is a deep bond between the hearts and minds of two people. God established this bond and created it for His glory. But it can be twisted, establishing an improper and toxic bond. In the case of the wife I counseled who seemed to have a soul tie to her former spouse, once that was identified and dealt with in prayer, she experienced major deliverance and freedom. The same is available to us! We can break soul ties and move forward in victory.

Soul ties are created through intimacy. People who engage in both emotional and physical intimacy outside the bonds of marriage create soul ties that can bring great destruction and havoc to their lives.

Soul ties can occur not just in the context of romantic relationships but also in the context of friendships and ministerial relationships. When you spend a great deal of time with a person and confide in them, you form a type of soul tie. There will be an emotional desire to be around that person, even if the person becomes destructive in your life.

> Or do you not know that he who is joined to a harlot is one body with her? For "the two," He says, "shall become one flesh." But he who is joined to the Lord is one spirit with Him. Flee sexual immorality. Every sin that a man does is outside the body, but he who commits sexual immorality sins against his own body.
>
> 1 Corinthians 6:16–18

One thing a sexual relationship outside of marriage does is that it establishes a soul tie. This will have you craving people who are toxic! During sexual intimacy, not only is an emotional tie formed with the other person, but also the demonic influences of all that person's previous partners can gain access to parts of your soul. This is one reason why people sometimes feel so confused and divided over their sexual history. Scripture teaches that this is the only sin against our own bodies (see 1 Corinthians 6:18). It has lasting repercussions in your body and mind.

Soul ties can also be formed by sharing the contents of your heart and most intimate thoughts. Samson shared the intimate details of his heart with Delilah, and it became his downfall!

> And it came to pass, when she pestered him daily with her words and pressed him, so that his soul was vexed to death, that he told her all his heart, and said to her, "No razor has ever come upon my head, for I have been a Nazirite to God from my mother's womb. If I am shaven, then my strength will leave me, and I shall become weak, and be like any other man."
>
> Judges 16:16–17

One spiritual mistake people may make is prematurely engaging in an inappropriate depth of either spiritual engagement or emotional communication with another person. For example, we may meet another prophetic person who speaks to our own undeveloped prophetic potential. Out of exuberance and excitement, we start having lengthy conversations with the person about our life's journey. Over time, we find ourselves knit to that person, with an unusual desire to communicate with them and stay connected. When God gives you a vision, steward it with wisdom and integrity. Your vision is not to be laid at everyone else's feet. It's intimate, personal, and holy unto the Lord. Be cautious about to whom you communicate the contents of your heart. This can create a bridge to disaster.

Symptoms of an Ungodly Soul Tie

Do you find yourself having deeply distressing feelings of detachment when you pull away from someone who is toxic? Is there dependence on the presence of another person or people that exceeds your devotion to the Lord? Do you constantly rely on others to provide your vision and strength, demonstrating little ability to steward it without other people? Are you drawn back to people who you know have destructive tendencies in your life? Do you find people invading your dreams and visions even when you've attempted to sever an unhealthy relationship? All these things are symptomatic of unhealthy soul ties.

Once you recognize an unhealthy soul tie, you must break it! Prayer is the key to breaking soul ties. Here is a prayer to break soul ties:

> *Father, I thank you for absolute freedom. I come before you now and bring every ungodly soul tie before your throne. I ask for your healing power to come forth. You are restoring my soul. You are healing my mind, will, and emotions right now. I invite the healing power of Jesus onto the scene. Come, mighty Holy Spirit, and*

release your healing power. I break any soul tie with _____ (insert name/names), in the name of Jesus. I command every yoke on my emotions to be broken off. I confess that I am free indeed! In the name of Jesus, Amen.

"I said, 'Lord, be merciful to me; heal my soul, for I have sinned against You'" (Psalm 41:4). Soul ties will draw you back toward a person who has been committing emotional manipulation and witchcraft in your life. Severing that soul tie and any emotional cords is imperative for your freedom and deliverance. Many times, you will have to pray again and again before you get to a complete release. You did not get into this entanglement overnight, and you may not get out of it overnight, either. But stick with finding your freedom in the name of Jesus!

The Power of Agreement and Alignment

"Can two walk together, except they are agreed?" (Amos 3:3). Agreement is one of the most powerful forces on earth. Understanding the power of agreement will upgrade your prayer life and kick-start your spiritual life! In our journey to shut the door on emotional witchcraft, we must look for areas where we have formed demonic agreements.

There is power in alignment. When God speaks a prophetic word to us, we align with it by coming into agreement with it. Third John 1:2 declares that it's the desire of the Lord for us to prosper and be in health even as our souls prosper. What does that look like? It's coming into alignment with the original intent of God for our lives. There is power when purpose, passion, and prophetic destiny align in our lives. We begin to live out our God-ordained purpose every day and uncap great joy and prosperity.

"Your kingdom come. Your will be done on earth as it is in heaven" (Matthew 6:10). One of the benefits of the prophetic realm is tuning in to the conversation in heaven. As we begin to understand what God is saying about our situation, our family, our assignment on earth, we are empowered to unlock the power and glory of God to fulfill that assignment. Agreement with heaven accesses the realm of God's supernatural power and brings it into manifestation on earth!

World changers are those who have heard from heaven and have chosen to align with heaven's decree. When we say "on earth as it is in heaven," we're talking not only about planet earth but also about the ground of our own hearts. We are inviting the heavenly realm to manifest in and through our lives, so that we may become like the apostle Peter, whose shadow started to do to people what God's shadow does. We become engulfed in the revelation, plan, and purposes of almighty God so completely that the heavenly realm is spilling out of us.

In each generation, there are people who come into such deep alignment with heaven that they shake their generation with the power of God! These are unusual people, charting unusual courses and doing unusual exploits. What has made them so unusual is their level of agreement with heaven. When you agree with God, you are unstoppable, because He is unstoppable.

What the devil wants to do is to get you out of agreement with God and ultimately in agreement with him, through lies, deception, and bondage! The attacks of the enemy against you are largely intended to diminish your prophetic sight and hearing. He wants to inundate you with false reports so he can captivate your attention and imagination. He wants you to think, dream, and see the dark possibilities of failure and bondage. It takes a settled heart and a made-up mind to boldly stand and tell the devil, "No!" Slamming demonic doors shut and exiting the cycle of control and manipulation requires you to stand firm in your authority. You can no longer agree with the lies of the enemy, and instead must come into agreement with the promises of God.

The Power of Words

Words are another powerful force in the realm of the spirit. "For by your words you will be justified, and by your words you will be condemned" (Matthew 12:37). When we hear the gospel of Jesus Christ and accept it, we then respond with the words of our mouth, appropriating the power of the gospel into our lives. Conversely, faith operates by being obtained in our hearts and then spoken by our mouths.

In the same manner, agreements with the devil are formed through first believing the enemy's report, and then speaking in alignment with what the enemy has said over our lives or a situation. Inner vows are demonic declarations and internal agreements that we've made during times of trial, trauma, and extreme adversity.

For example, I remember the story of a prophet who had been rejected by his church in a very painful way. His leaders had warned him not to allow anyone into his inner circle. He came into agreement with that instruction, and so made a vow to be distant from everybody. While there is wisdom in protecting yourself from the wrong relationships, a vow like this can be demonic, because it ultimately withholds the ability to receive the right relationships God sends to you and keeps you trapped in dark isolation.

Breaking Demonic Inner or Verbal Vows

I want you to do a heart check and examine whether you have come into agreement with the enemy in any area or if you have made an inner vow that is limiting you. Seek the Holy Spirit's guidance to reveal any inner vows you've made. Common demonic vows are vowing never to trust again, or pronouncing a curse over yourself like, *I can't do that. I'm not able.* It is believing a lie and then coming into alignment with it! Such vows create demonic doorways and access points. Spiritual agreements are pacts or covenants that are knowingly or unknowingly made with the enemy. They grant him legal access to your life! Coming out of agreement with these demonic vows is imperative for your spiritual and emotional success.

When we have aligned our hearts with the lies of the enemy, we often make verbal vows. Verbal vows are demonic pronunciations that we have spoken in agreement with the report of the enemy! They become habitations for demonic entities to torment and harass us. We spoke the words in a time of crisis or calamity, but in fact, we agreed with the report of hell and we must now come out of agreement with it. These are spiritual decrees that have been based on negative experiences, pain, or trauma.

How do we break both inner vows and verbal vows? We must do it by changing our beliefs, coming out of agreement, and then renouncing the vow that has been made! According to Webster's online dictionary, the word *renounce* means "to give up, refuse, or resign usually by formal declaration."[1] So in this case we must say aloud, "I renounce any inner vows I made with the enemy," and then speak the things from our mouths that we've agreed with in our hearts that are demonic lies. We must also say aloud, "I renounce every vow I made, such as (whatever things we have previously said that the Holy Spirit has now convicted us of)."

We came into agreement by believing a lie, making a vow based on that lie, and speaking that vow aloud. Now we come out of agreement by believing and speaking the opposite! We release the power of blessing by speaking the opposite of what the enemy has spoken over us, after we have formally renounced the vow. We then come into a time of repentance, asking the Lord to forgive us, and calling forth His presence over our lives in that area. We find and memorize Scripture that speaks God's truth to those lies.

Breaking Free from Limiting Mindsets

As we continue our freedom journey, it's also important that we examine any limiting thoughts or mindsets we have adopted. These are lies we have believed based on negative aspects of where we came from and what we have been through in our lives. Often in times of crisis and trauma, we adopt a limiting belief system that causes us to believe there is an invisible lid over our lives. Limiting belief systems are mental constraints formed by demonic lies that hinder our ability to fully embrace the life that God has designed for us. These beliefs act as barriers, preventing us from achieving our prophetic potential and experiencing the reality of God's plan for us.

In the Bible, we see that God has created each of us with a unique plan and purpose and has endowed us with divine ability and talent to glorify Him (see Jeremiah 29:11). However, when we believe lies about our identity, capabilities, and worth, we place an invisible but ever-present mental lid on our lives that keeps us from doing the kingdom exploits God ordained for us. Limiting mindsets show up in many ways. They include doubts about our abilities and purpose, and even negative views about our personality. They also try to disrupt our ability to believe God's goodness in our lives.

The children of Israel exhibited such a limiting mindset when they bowed to fear about entering the promised land, despite God's promise of victory. They said, "We are not able to go up against the people, for they are stronger than we" (Numbers 13:31). Their belief in this lie led to their failure to embrace what the Lord said, and they never entered the land God had promised them. Lies are sent to cripple your faith and crush your progress! Demonic pronouncements are one primary way the enemy seeks to steal, kill, and destroy (see John 10:10). The devil is described as the "father of lies" (John 8:44), and he works overtime to plant seeds of doubt and deceit in our minds. The goal is to keep us away from God's truth.

Such lies may be subtle, such as believing you are unworthy of love. Or they may be more overt, such as thinking that your past sins disqualify you from God's grace in your life today. The Bible assures you that you are "fearfully and wonderfully made" (Psalm 139:14), and that "there is therefore now no condemnation to them which are in Christ Jesus"

(Romans 8:1), and this includes you! You are walking in the grace of God, and His mercy for you is new today. Therefore, every accusation from your past is currently irrelevant; if you have been forgiven, it is under the blood of Jesus.

Breaking free from limiting beliefs requires a conscious and persistent effort to align your thoughts with God's Word. The apostle Paul instructs us to "be transformed by the renewing of your mind" (Romans 12:2). This renewal comes through immersing ourselves in Scripture, which reveals our real identity, future promises, and present help. When faced with evil lies, we counter them with the truth of God's Word!

For example, when we feel incapable and unqualified, we can declare, "I can do all things through Christ who strengthens me" (Philippians 4:13). By continually speaking and meditating on God's Word, we kick-start our faith! We also dismantle the strongholds of limiting beliefs and replace them with His truth. Faith is believing. This means standing on the side of heaven. If God said it, it's true and the devil is a liar! When we boldly dig our heels into the promises of God and the reality of His Word for our lives, we are empowered to soar. We break through limiting belief systems, and we embrace the plan and the purpose of God to move forward in the grace that is abundantly available for our lives.

Five Types of Dangerous Relationships

Here are five types of dangerous relationships that will hinder your destiny. They are what I call *rebel relationships, diminishing relationships, impure relationships, soulish relationships*, and *pain partners*. These types of relationships are very dangerous because they can counteract your prophetic purpose and destiny. When God assigns you to something that is bigger than where you are today, He will bring in bigger people with bigger ideas and bigger voices. These powerful, positive people will sharpen you and at times aggressively confront areas in you that need reformation and change. If you yield to what is most comfortable, however, you will instead choose to align with other broken people in relationships that are dangerous to you. These alignments will hinder your growth. Let's look at each of the five types of dangerous relationships a little more closely.

1. Rebel relationships. Part of surrendering to God's plan is surrendering to His process. The enemy will send people into your life who offer you a shortcut and will affirm rebellion in your heart, instead of speaking to the consecration that is necessary for the highest level of God's purpose to manifest in your life. Beware of those who confirm your rebellion and continually counsel you to ignore the voices of solid friends, concerned family members, and skilled leaders! These relationships steer you away from purpose, accountability, and healthy communication. They reinforce your negative characteristics, fleshly outbursts, and toxic behaviors. They are formed by a dangerous familiarity—it "feels right" for all the wrong reasons!

2. Diminishing relationships. These relationships are formed with insecure people. They demand that you water yourself down to be more palatable to them. They do not encourage your forward motion and continual growth; instead, they desire for you to sink back into the old ways and patterns God is bringing you out of. When you press for goals within the context of these relationships, the other party will get angry! Your desire to do more and achieve more speaks to their stagnation. They control you by attempting to accuse and attack you in a way that diminishes your potential for growth. Ultimately, they're trying to keep you on their level and despise the fact that you have a hunger for something more. If you do not confront and exit this type of relationship, you will end up submitting your growth to their dysfunction and you will be stagnated.

3. *Impure relationships.* This is a type of relationship that attempts to link you to past behaviors, thoughts, mindsets, and bondages that will contaminate your future destiny and present reality. These are formed through familiar spirits that draw you to people who carry the sinful nature God either has brought you out of or is offering to release you from. For example, if you are being delivered from lust, there may be a relationship with another person who has a strong measure of lust working in their life. It will feel very familiar and therefore cause a level of comfort to be present that leads you back to bondage. This type of relationship will lull you into the sin that you have been pressing to be free from. It is a draw to a person that shares your proclivity and bondage. It can enter very subtly and deceptively. This is where accountability is critical. Be aware that if you are being sucked into this kind of danger, you will likely get angry about warnings others give you regarding the relationship.

Also remember that deliverance requires guardrails! What do I mean by this? It's quite simple. You must enforce the reality of what God has said about you, and override the past behavior patterns you learned in demonic habitations. Once you cast the devil out, you must then deal with both the appetite and the mindset. Guardrails are critically important to keep you on track. This includes your prayer life, your study and meditation time, your church attendance, your community involvement, and your emotional and spiritual development. It also includes your relationships. If you're going to live a consecrated life, your relationships will also need to be consecrated!

4. *Soulish relationships.* Let me be clear about this type of relationship. We are intended to connect with other people emotionally and spiritually. It is part of our human existence and our journey with God and His people. But these types of relationships are rooted solely in a soulish familiarity and comfort. There is no spiritual root system or depth within the relationship; it is formed with those who provide a quick boost but don't have spiritual depth. These soulish relationships become a huge distraction because they do not value spiritual growth or pursuing divine goals. Instead, they speak to your current comfort. Comfort is the enemy of growth! The areas in which we grow are uncomfortable. Olympic athletes are up early and stay awake late at night with a directed diet so they can dedicate themselves to the utmost level of physical training. They cannot spend their time with a person or people who claim that their rigorous routine is too difficult and that they should abandon it. They have a goal in mind; therefore, their whole lives are about stewarding that goal well.

The truth is, every prophetic promise will require both partnership and stewardship. Partnership is the acceptance and agreement of the promise. Stewardship speaks of management. In the context of prophetic destiny, stewardship is the management of our time, our devotional life, our prayers, our spiritual development, and our relationships. Far too many people think they can delegate and outsource their development to someone else. But we must take our development personally, and these types of soulish relationships will not only limit development but also contradict it. These types of people will speak to our fleshly desires and ultimately lull us to sleep instead of pursuing our prophetic destiny.

5. *Pain partners.* This is a type of relationship that connects people in an unhealthy way through shared pain and trauma. It is extremely dangerous, because the bond is built in toxicity. The other party affirms your bad behaviors and does not speak to the areas of your life that need growth. You will stay bound in this type of alignment. There is no sharpening or spiritual growth. Pain partners also fuel your bad behaviors by affirming your lack of accountability. They identify with the broken parts of your soul and personality, thereby agreeing with unhealthy mindsets and resulting actions.

A vivid example of a pain partnership took place between a highly prophetic younger woman and an older woman who served as a mother figure. The younger had been through extreme rejection in a very dysfunctional family. She had a potent prophetic calling and was very sensitive to environments and atmospheres. She also had a sharp gift of discernment. But she lacked grace with people, and tended to lash out emotionally whenever there was conflict on any level. Additionally, she dealt with rebellion and was inconsistent in submission to leadership and maintaining healthy ministry relationships. When a challenge would arise, she would declare that she had heard from God—and bail! She entered churches loudly, and then could be quite boisterous on the way out!

This young lady met the older woman, and they immediately connected. The older viewed her like a daughter and affirmed her in areas that brought much comfort to her soul. As the two began to be involved in ministry together, they would create issues in which they could rebel against the leader, while comforting and affirming each other. It became a toxic bond that reinforced their negative behaviors. Instead of helping each other to heal, they further encouraged one another's dysfunction in the name of love! Their relationship would cause them to breach ministerial protocols and avoid ethical decisions. They finally got into a situation where there was confrontation with leaders at a ministry to which they were both submitted. During that time, they chose secrecy and mutual affirmation over healthy conflict resolution and responsibility. Both ended up leaving God-ordained posts and positions because of mutual pain. They were unable to sharpen each other or help each other process in a healthy way. Instead, they pledged undying loyalty and were voices of unhealthy agreement one to the other.

Align with the Right People

It's time to break agreement with the enemy in every area of our lives, including our relationships. Each of us has a prophetic destiny that is unique to our own personality and gifting. Part of our process is God sending the right people into our lives and helping us grow together. Choosing alignment with broken people and refusing to grow is a dangerous, life-altering decision! You will stay at the level of growth where you are, instead of maximizing your God-given destiny and assignment. To grow supernaturally and in every positive way, align with the right people in godly relationships.

Here are some questions to reflect on after reading this chapter: *What lies about myself have I believed? What limiting mindsets do I need to leave behind? What inner or verbal vows do I need to break? Are there soul ties that are hindering my journey with God? What types of toxic alignments have I formed?*

Confronting these issues and coming out of agreement with them will position you to maximize your prophetic destiny. You will move up higher, and you will slam internal doors shut to demonic lies, manipulation, and emotional witchcraft.

ooooooooooooo **LET'S REFLECT** ooooooooooooo

1. List three ways a soul tie can be formed.
2. What steps can you take to align with a prophetic word from God?
3. What is an example of a limiting mindset? What ways can you use to break free from it?
4. Of the five types of dangerous relationships, which one do you relate to most? Is this relationship current? What will you do about it?

CHAPTER EIGHT

Growing Relationally

We've spent a lot of time talking about the potential for toxicity in relationships, but we must also explore the value of meaningful spiritual relationships. I want to go all the way back to the Garden of Eden, the origination of our story. In the Garden, God created Adam to commune with Him. There was no wall of separation between God and man; their relationship was unhindered. Even though there was this glorious communion between the Creator and the creation, there was still an absence in the heart of Adam: "And the LORD God said, 'It is not good that man should be alone; I will make him a helper comparable to him'" (Genesis 2:18).

This is an extremely complex human condition. Adam enjoyed the magnificent presence of God on a continual basis, but part of his humanity still longed for human connection. As a man, there was part of his manhood that needed to be connected to a soul mate. His mind, his will, and his emotions craved the presence of another human. God answered this dilemma by creating woman to walk alongside man in the endeavors of life. This is not a problematic or toxic situation, but a glorious union that unfolds a picture of the love of God toward humanity. God wanted to give Adam a helper suited to him, and created Eve to walk alongside him.

We can sometimes wrestle with the reality that we are spiritual beings and should feel satisfied with the presence of God alone, yet we are also human beings. This means that humanity and divinity meet like a crossroads in our lives. We are not less spiritual because we desire human connection, whether in a romantic relationship, a friendship, or the assembling of ourselves together in a church body. It's not an "either-or" proposition, but a "both-and." Humans were made to connect one to another, but there are different reasons for connecting. There are different types of relationships that are part of our human experience, and the desire to have human connection is not evil. But it can lead you down a wrong road if you are not wise in the way you connect.

Warning signs and critical pieces of information concerning wrong relationships are needed, but they are only half of the picture. There are also rich and vital relationships that will bring great strength to your life! I've been told that when agents are being trained to spot counterfeit money, they don't study a fake; they spend their time studying real currency. When they can identify the real, they can quickly spot the counterfeit. I would submit to you that we must take a similar view concerning relationships. We need to understand the value of them and the necessity they hold in our lives so that we can then identify that which is unhealthy or toxic.

The Support of Friendship

To properly appreciate and manage our relationships, we must first define them. I've always said that what you fail to define will fail in your life. Everything in your life demands definition. For example, I need to know the difference between a personal errand and a work assignment. If I categorize them as the same thing, I will ultimately fail at work and face the consequences.

So let's think of relationships in the form of a ladder. Different types of relationships fulfill different roles in our complex human journey. Once we properly understand the needs of these relationships, we can then provide assessments about their health. Let's begin first with one of the most common relationships we all need—friendship. A friend is on a very specific assignment: to support, to love, and to be an unwavering presence in life. The proof of friendship is consistency. People teach you what they value by their consistency.

I once had an experience where somebody continually did not show up for me. Each time the person didn't show up, a logical excuse was given for not showing up. But after a string of these episodes, it finally dawned on me that I was not a priority to the person. The person felt an obligation to provide an excuse, but the reality is, the person's time management proved his priorities. I notified this person that even though I appreciated him providing me input, I recognized that his choices showed his values and that he wasn't valuing the relationship on the level that he'd expressed verbally. Sometimes when people express their support with words, their actions speak something else.

"A friend loves at all times, and a brother is born for adversity" (Proverbs 17:17). Support is one of the most beautiful aspects of friendship. A good, godly friend supports your values and your faith. The person won't be trying to talk you into doing crazy things and going back to lifestyle choices God delivered you from. A good friend's level of support is not just spiritual, however; it's intrinsically emotional. The person is in your cheerleading section, there to support you in your ups and downs, your mountains and valleys, consistent in love and emotional support.

At the core of every relationship is sacrifice. "Greater love has no one than this, than to lay down one's life for his friends" (John 15:13). Those who paint pictures of easy friendship are giving you only half the story. The truth is, there's going to be a tremendous amount of sacrificial giving; a good friend makes sacrifices for a friend. One way we identify healthy friendships is through their commitment to our lives. It should never be a one-way commitment; that's a danger sign in a friendship. If I'm always supporting you and you're never supporting me, that reveals emotional manipulation. You have manipulated me to gain access to me, but you've proven not to be a reliable friend.

Here's one thing we need to understand about friendships: Each one has an assignment. A friend's assignment is to navigate all the varying seasons of life with unwavering support, loyalty, and honesty. Friends will say the difficult things, but they will say those things in love. The goal of a friendship is not so much your growth and development as it is enjoying the journey of life together. Let me say it this way: A friend loves you just the way you are, but a mentor loves you too much to leave you the way you are. The assignment of a mentor is growth, and the assignment of a friend is support. They are both critically important relationships, but they play different roles.

The Covenant of Marriage

"Therefore a man shall leave his father and mother and be joined to his wife, and they will become one flesh" (Genesis 2:24). Other than our relationship with God, the union of marriage is the most consecrated relationship in life. It is the only place, relationally, where two literally become one. God designed the human anatomy to unite in a way within the context of marriage that is intended to tie two people together.

This relationship is a covenant relationship. It involves a tremendous amount of sacrifice. In fact, love is proven through sacrifice. If we are thinking of relationships in the category of assignments, marriage is of the highest priority. This is the reason the apostle Paul said that singleness served him well in his apostolic assignment. He understood that if he'd had a spouse, he would have had to sacrifice for that spouse. Making the decision to marry a person who supports your destiny and your call from God comes with high stakes. I've seen many young, called people marry a person who did not support that destiny, and shipwreck followed.

"Husbands, love your wives, just as Christ also loved the church and gave Himself for her" (Ephesians 5:25). Men are created as warriors, champions, and protectors. There's a fierce nature that God put in the soul of a man to provide a sacrificial covering for his amazing wife. Conversely, women carry a sensitivity, a birthing, and an intercessory capacity that has the potential to elevate a man to places beyond where he could walk alone. When these two come together in total unity, it creates an unprecedented momentum. It has been said that behind every strong man is a great woman, and I believe it's true!

I know some of you may take exception to the descriptions I've given, because we're living in an era that wants to diminish the individuality of men and women. Don't get me wrong—I was raised by a single mom and she's one of the strongest people I've ever known! Women have their own fierce nature that complements that of a man in an amazing way. When these two come together, the foundation is love! Paul was admonishing husbands to go to a depth and a level of sacrifice in a marriage relationship that will model the ultimate expression of Christ's love for the church. God deemed this sacrifice beautiful and necessary in our journeys!

If we're thinking in context of importance, this relationship must take the highest priority, after our relationship with God. I always say it this way: If I'm not properly vertically aligned with God, I'll never be properly horizontally aligned with anyone else. My marriage comes before my ministry. My marriage comes before my children. I know some may take exception with that as well, but the truth is, if you have an unstable marriage, you'll have an unstable family. Before there were children, there were a husband and a wife, a man and a woman, two lovers becoming one. The bedrock of the family is the marriage. That's why the enemy wants to redefine marriage and tear down the role of man and woman, male and female. He hates God's creation and God's intended purpose for you and me!

Honoring and Respecting Leadership

"Obey those who rule over you, and be submissive, for they watch out for your souls, as those who must give account. Let them do so with joy and not with grief, for that would be unprofitable for you" (Hebrews 13:17). God has invested portions of His grace and power in human vessels. He's the originator of the concept of leadership.

We can look to the Old Testament and see how God anointed Moses to lead Israel out of Egyptian bondage. We can see how God called Elijah to confront the false prophets of his day. God sent Jeremiah with the weeping word to a backslidden nation. In the New Testament, God anointed Peter as one of the fathers of the early church and used him to preach the inaugural message out of the upper room! God then raised up Paul after his Damascus Road experience.

We are living in a day and an hour where authority is despised! But we must understand there is no authority that has not been established by God. A pastor, spiritual leader, or overseer is sent to your life to bring the kingdom and the power of God to you. When we begin to form a relationship with a spiritual leader that we confuse with a friendship, we will mishandle the relationship. I'm not stating that spiritual leaders should not be kind or walk in love, but their presence in your life has a different assignment from a friend's assignment.

The words I quoted from Hebrews might make us say ouch! But the Bible declares that there are leaders who are placed over us. His anointing flows from the head down to every facet of our lives. This doesn't mean that leaders hold any special salvation. It's simply speaking of their position of leadership within the body of Christ. Through honor and respect, we handle those relationships righteously; from them, we gain valuable insight and strength.

Questions to Ask in Stewarding Relationships

As we begin to learn the roles that different relationships play in our lives, it empowers us to steward those relationships well. Many times, what we might think is warfare is simply a result of immaturity. We respond to a disagreement through brokenness instead of peace. We turn a different point of view into an unnecessary argument. Or perhaps we're triggered from previous trauma, so we prematurely exit a relationship that was brought to us to give a better understanding of God's purpose for our lives.

Our examination must begin with evaluation. The first question we must ask ourselves is, *Who am I?* You see, your life is complex. Think of it as a tapestry with various parts of your human experience interwoven. You are the total of your experiences and the way you've chosen to respond to them. Did you learn the lessons that were necessary in the times of trial? Are you still sitting by the roadside because of a painful experience, instead of getting back into this race called life? Did you decide never to open your heart to anybody else because of previous pain?

Why are these questions important? The answer is simple. How can I relate to you if I don't properly know *me*? I found that one of the gifts of counseling is gaining perspective. Oftentimes, we've deceived ourselves about who we are, and it's not until somebody shares an honest and unbiased perspective that we gain necessary insight.

"Investigate my life, O God, find out everything about me; cross-examine and test me, get a clear picture of what I'm about; see for yourself whether I've done anything wrong—then guide me on the road to eternal life" (Psalm 139:23–24 MSG). One way to do a good self-examination is to ask the Holy Spirit to shine His spotlight on your heart. Invite Him to reveal parts of yourself that you may have overlooked or that have been unknown to you. Spend time in contemplative prayer and stillness before the Lord. Spend time thinking about your journey, and ask the Lord what lessons you needed to learn that perhaps you did not learn. Ask God to illuminate your stewardship of relationships, friendships, and connections. If you truly yield yourself to this process, God will be faithful to reveal things you've probably not seen before.

The next question needs to be, *Where am I?* You see, life is divided into a series of seasons. I'm moving in a different rhythm today than I did in my twenties. I value things today that I overlooked in my early days of ministry. I have changed as the seasons have changed. This is part of life's growth process. "To everything there is a season, a time to every purpose under heaven" (Ecclesiastes 3:1). Learning which season you're in and what your personal needs are will help position you to properly manage your relationships.

Sometimes, as your season shifts and your assignment evolves, your relationships need to change. We've heard it said that Abraham could not take everybody up to the mountain. Neither could Jesus take all His disciples into the home of Jairus. It's true. Evaluating your present season and location will guide you in stewarding your relationships. You should never feel guilty about growth! Any relationship that demands you stop growing to stay in the relationship is dangerous. Your true friends, family, fellow church members, and spiritual leaders should all be championing growth in your life! But those who operate in emotional manipulation may be intimidated by your growth. As you advance in discernment, you will begin to see their wicked ways and uncover their maneuvers. They don't want your eyes to be opened; therefore, they will try to oppress you and keep you distracted and confused!

Growth is a gift of life, but it is also a choice! When you go through a season of great difficulty, you have the choice to be still and listen to God in that season or to embrace bitterness. It is within your human capacity to choose which road you will take. Each season holds both beauty and value, but some seasons just require more searching to find them. Maturity finds the footprints of God in every season! You need relationships that reinforce and celebrate your growth. You need growth champions in your life who are partnering with God's intended plan and purpose for you. Also, you need those who will love you enough to correct you when you begin to speak against the planned purpose and destiny of God for your life! You need accountability partners.

The question also needs to be asked, *In what areas of growth in my own life is God dealing with me?* As you advance in your purpose, God is going to highlight spaces that require growth. These spaces will demand the presence of the right people in your life. For example, if you're trying to grow in business, you may need a skilled business mentor. If you're trying to grow in prophetic understanding and function, you may need teaching that helps equip you for that. This doesn't mean you throw out your previous relationships; rather, you make room for some new ones by adding space to your life. Your relationships should match your journey.

Emotional and Relational Intelligence

Emotions are beautiful gifts through which we experience the highs and lows of life. We are not to vilify our emotions, but we are to properly manage them. "He who is slow to anger is better than the mighty, and he who rules his spirit than he that takes a city" (Proverbs 16:32). This Scripture speaks about the importance of managing anger instead of being overcome by it.

Emotional intelligence plays an important role in our relationship skills. Emotional intelligence refers to our ability to understand, recognize, manage, and influence our own emotions and the emotions of others. It's a vital skill for our personal, professional, and ministerial success.

Emotional intelligence involves five key components:

- *Self-awareness*, our ability to recognize and understand our own strengths, weaknesses, emotions, and values.
- *Self-regulation*, our ability to manage our emotions and corresponding actions in a healthy way.
- *Motivation*, our ability to work hard, have a positive attitude, and impact others around us in a productive way.
- *Social skills*, our ability to properly manage relationships in our lives, helping people move into desired directions, communicating effectively, and building rich interpersonal connections.

- *Empathy*, our ability to understand, validate, and share the feelings of others, while being sensitive to their concerns and needs.

Jesus' ministry in healing our souls can provide a rich template for balance in healthy emotional intelligence. Counseling, therapy, and deliverance are also tools that will help us break free from demonic entanglements and old soul wounds so that our emotional intelligence grows in healthier ways.

We also need to understand *relational intelligence*, which is our ability to successfully navigate and manage relationships with others. It hinges on the ability to understand and effectively interact with various types of personalities in different contexts. Here are key components of relational intelligence:

- *The ability to understand others*, which includes perceiving their emotions, intentions, motivations, and behaviors from a healthy place.
- *Interpersonal skills*, skills that help us to communicate effectively and create a positive and cooperative environment, while resolving conflicts in a mature manner.
- *Building trust* with the people around us through consistency and honesty in our relational activities. We've got to be adaptable to various changes of seasons and relationships.

We need to do an honest evaluation about the status of our own emotional and relational intelligence. Are there areas in which our relationships are suffering because we're just not mature in these spaces? Is Jesus inviting us into a journey of learning how to sacrificially love and serve others? Do we have more room to grow in our relationships? If the answer to these questions is yes, then the next question to ask ourselves becomes, *To what steps have I committed in order to grow?*

I want you to be very intentional about prioritizing healthy relationships. I'm glad that we're on a journey to expose and disempower emotional manipulation in our lives! By discovering the attributes of toxic relationships, we can avoid them or correct them. Yet we also need to know and understand the value of rich and life-giving relationships, and invest ourselves properly in them.

Things That Damage Relationships

One of the things that will often damage our relationships is having unrealistic expectations. We may do this because we're looking to plug an emotional hole. But then, we place a responsibility on another human that no one is able to fulfill.

For example, as a leader I have often had people come into my life who had experienced damaged parental relationships. They falsely believed that my presence in their life would heal the absence of their parent. The reality is that a spiritual parent never fills a void created by the absence of a biological parent. The only pathway to healing is the presence of God, who heals and carefully tends our hearts. Putting that expectation on another human sets up the relationship for failure, right out of the gate.

Another very damaging attribute is overcommitting out of a fear of rejection. Sometimes we want so deeply to be loved that we'll say yes to everything, and then we find ourselves running ragged, trying to satisfy the needs of others. We do so in a quest to be loved and accepted and to fill some childhood wound, but it only leads us to exhaustion. Are you overcommitting in your relationships? Have you done a deep dive into the spirit of rejection as a result? Have you realized the vast and glorious gift of the love and acceptance of God in your life?

Distance from God also damages our relationships. The centrality of our success in human relationships hinges upon our own devotion to Jesus. How can I properly love you if I'm not spending quality time with God? Truly, it's impossible. When I'm in prayer, I'm a better husband. When I'm in devotion, I'm a better father. When I'm spending time with the Lord, I'm a better leader. There's just no shortcut—we need the sustaining presence of God in every part of our lives!

Jesus Is the Relational Standard

"Pattern yourselves after me [follow my example], as I imitate and follow Christ (the Messiah)" (1 Corinthians 11:1 AMPC). Jesus is the standard! He is the pinnacle of success and perfect example of godly living. The apostle Paul made the point of telling the church at Corinth that they were to follow him only as he was following Christ Jesus. Paul had to first be personally devoted to the cause of Christ. He had to have a red-hot prayer life, which we know he did by his writings to this church. He had a strong devotional life, which empowered him to be victorious in his leadership with those who were relating to him in that capacity.

I can't remember a time in my early married life when I wasn't struggling to be a good husband. Yet I spent a lot of my time focusing on what I perceived were my wife's shortcomings! One day in prayer, the Lord told me to stop praying about what I thought was wrong with my wife and start praying over my own heart and role as a husband. God began to bring deep conviction about areas in which I needed to draw closer to Him. He allowed me to see that me being a godly husband was as spiritual as preaching to the nations. Over time, He dealt with the inner parts of my heart and began to bring healing and revelation to me. Everything in my life and marriage changed as I went on that journey with God.

Perhaps your relationships with your spouse or children are suffering because God is inviting you into spaces of relationship with Him and you've not yet gone. Perhaps relationships with spiritual leaders are suffering because you've not yet gone to the depths of where God wants to take you in Him. Our relationship with God will define every other relationship in our lives. It ends and begins at the cross, spending time with our risen Savior!

We need to understand these truths: Relationships are necessary, valuable, constantly moving, and sometimes messy! Understand that you need human connection; it's not an expression of a weakness. Once you accept that truth, you're empowered to invest properly in right relationships, and exit wrong ones.

I also want you to focus on the fact that good relationships add value to *you*. They may be few, but embracing quality over quantity is very important. I said that relationships are sometimes messy, and I know you might not like that, but it's simply true. They are messy because we bring our humanity into them. We bring our emotions, our past pain, and troubles. Successful relationships must be based on acceptance. Jesus accepted us in our brokenness and provided healing. Good relationships accept our humanity and champion our growth. A healthy relationship does a lot less judging and a lot more loving. There will be ups and downs, and there will be mountains and valleys, but along the way there will also be opportunities to love better and learn more.

Here are some questions for reflection as you respond to what you have read in this chapter: *Where do I need to grow in defining relationships? What is the status of my relational and emotional intelligence? Have I properly invested in my relationships? Have I allowed past experiences to cloud my current relationships? What steps am I taking to heal?*

Without intentionality about growing relationally and stewarding your relationships, you will remain stuck!

LET'S REFLECT

1. Do your friendships have definition? If not, take time to determine their place and function in your life.
2. What is your assignment in the lives of your closest friends?
3. One key component of relational intelligence is maintaining consistency and honesty. In what ways can you strengthen your level of consistency and honesty in your relationships?

4. This chapter contains a section on things that damage relationships. Review that list and choose one attribute that you notice within yourself and make a strategy to actively work on it this month.

CHAPTER NINE

Healing Emotionally

The Spirit of the Lord is upon Me, because He has anointed Me to preach the gospel to the poor; He has sent me to heal the brokenhearted, to proclaim liberty to the captives and recovery of sight to the blind, to set at liberty those who are oppressed.

Luke 4:18

In this inaugural sermon of Jesus' ministry, He reveals one of the most beautiful parts of His character. He states that the Spirit of the Lord is upon Him to heal the brokenhearted. This is what I call "heart healing." We're not talking about our physical hearts, but our emotional hearts—the part of our being that makes decisions, processes memories, and houses our moral compass. Jesus can transform the most broken of hearts and the most ravaged of souls. I love the fact that when we come to acknowledge Jesus as Savior, we surrender our spirit, our soul, and our body to Him. There is no part of us that is off limits to Him! He knows the depth of our pain and the wonder of our most audacious dreams. As we've been on this journey of slamming the door shut to emotional witchcraft, manipulative friends, and demonic control, we've also considered the importance of our own emotional health.

This brings me to a very vivid memory. I was young and newly saved when the Lord thrust me into ministry. I would say that I was the least likely candidate to be used of God as a preacher. After all, my life began surrounded by sin and bondage. I was broken, ashamed, and filled with all types of demonic lies. I was exhilarated just to be in the house of the Lord. I never imagined that He would have a desire to use my broken life as a testimony of His goodness and redemption. It was with that in mind that I went off to Bible college. I arrived at that powerful school of ministry still in the beginnings of my deliverance journey. One of the first things I observed was how so many of the instructors and guest speakers were filled with the power of God in a way I had not seen before. The church I was going to before I left for my cross-country adventure to Bible college was a nice community church with kind leaders, but there was no intense flow of the raw power of God.

During this season in my life, I was also seeing prophetic ministry up close, along with mighty deliverance ministry. One of the ministers I came across had an unusual ability to sense and see what was going on in the lives of people. I was fascinated by this and then later realized it was because a major part of my calling was the prophetic as well. Sometimes God will allow us to see something that inspires the part of our destiny that is not yet fulfilled. This leader was an inspiration to me as I watched him move in the power of

God in an unusual way. I was drawn to his prophetic insight, his boldness and his accuracy! I saw the impact it was having on others around him, and I wanted to learn more about the type of prophetic ministry in which he engaged.

Over the process of time, the Lord allowed me to observe that leader closely. He was a powerful man of God filled with wisdom, but beneath the surface were some lingering problems. I started to observe some extremely unhealthy tendencies that gave way to control and manipulation. This challenged my young mind, because I wrongly assumed that everyone God used had it all together. Wow, did I have a lot to learn!

God has a way of taking broken vessels and pouring some of His most potent oil through them. The fact that we are anointed does not disqualify us from having character issues! This is a lesson I had to learn the hard way. As I saw the control that was operating through this man, my mind raced to try to figure out what was going on. After all, how could he be so anointed and so bound at the same time? I would go so far as to say that I believe the man had a Jezebel spirit operating through him. I know that's an audacious thing to say, and I did not arrive at that conclusion lightly.

I quickly learned that I had to use healthy boundaries in my involvement with this person. In the early stages, I was not very successful because I had way too much brokenness in myself. It was difficult for me at times to say no to him as we got to know each other. Over time, however, I learned that without saying no, that Jezebel spirit would kick the door down and take over every part of my life. This was something I simply couldn't have! But I struggled to search for answers.

How could this man be so anointed and profound, yet so very bound at the same time?

As I got to know him as a person, he shared parts of his story with me that began to fill in the blanks. He had an extremely difficult childhood and struggled to feel loved and accepted. Being thrust into the ministry put him in a position where people were constantly coming and going. He often struggled, as many ministers do, with feeling unloved. We make the mistake of thinking if somebody leaves our church, it's automatically a personal issue. How can it not be personal when it's the church we built that represents us? This is one thing that leaders will have to wrestle with—you may think you built the church, but it was God. People come and go, but your mission remains the same. There must be a healthy grieving process, as well as honest evaluation. Sometimes people scream that they love you and they're going to stay with you forever, only to leave soon after! It's one of the very fragile human conditions we deal with in the kingdom of God.

This man had a soul that had been ravaged by layer upon layer of rejection and pain. He had never found a way to properly deal with it. I watched as God sent prophets and concerned people to his life to try to help him in his healing. Time and time again, he would get offended when they shared with him his need for healing. He was unwilling to be vulnerable, and the truth is, healing and deliverance require a level of both humility and vulnerability. To make an extremely long story short, the man stayed stuck in his bondage. It was a great lesson to me in my early days of ministry. I realized that you can indeed be highly anointed and highly broken at the same time. Healing is a choice! Just as the sick person goes down to an altar for healing prayer, so must the person struggling in their emotions open their heart to the power of God to heal. He is ready, willing, and able to heal the depths of our emotions.

Green Pastures and Quiet Pools

"God, my shepherd! I don't need a thing. You have bedded me down in lush meadows, you find me quiet pools to drink from. True to your word, you let me catch my breath and send me in the right direction" (Psalm 23:1–3 msg). Jesus is the Good Shepherd! I love this psalm and all the benefits that are listed within it. One of the things God does is lead the sheep to lush meadows. Other translations say "green pastures." What do green pastures represent for sheep? They represent a place of abundance. If we read on, it says that He gives us "quiet pools to drink from," which represent peace and tranquility. Jesus as the Good Shepherd leads our souls away from the rejection and pain we've known in the past. He brings us to the space of healing and acceptance in His love. There is no part of our human process or struggle He overlooks. He desires to be involved in every intricate detail of our human affairs and life.

The Good Shepherd expresses undying and unwavering concern for us. We are His sheep and He is our shepherd. His goal is to lead us into the fullness of who He is and all that He has. Heaven is a place of peace and abundance. Heaven is a place where there is no fretting or despair, and the more that we relate to the Lord, the more that we will relate to His healing power. To conceal our pain is to empower the bondage. If we keep the thing covered, it's because we are too proud to admit we need the help of the Lord!

Pride empowers demonic operations. Healing is the portion of the humble! The acknowledgment of our need for Jesus, the healer of our soul, is the first step to recovery. Perhaps we look back at our journey and see continual missteps because of anxiety or fear. Or maybe we can look at the effects of depression that caused us to sink into despair that feels like a cloudy day that never ends. Maybe we wrestle with the disappointment of a failed dream or an unmet desire. All those things can be healed in the presence of God.

> Is anyone among you sick? Let him call for the elders of the church, and let them pray over him, anointing him with oil in the name of the Lord. And the prayer of faith will save the sick, and the Lord will raise him up. And if he has committed sins, he will be forgiven.
>
> James 5:14–15

Notice that healing demands pursuit from the sick. In these verses, it says let the sick call for the elders of the church. That call is an admission that the sick one needs help. It works the same way in heart healing and soul healing. We call for the Great Shepherd of our souls to come into the broken places and spaces and bring healing. This is the call of sons and daughters to cry out to the Father and say, "Daddy, I need you."

When it comes to the healing process, we must begin with the understanding that all healing begins and ends with the Lord Jesus. No matter what kind of work we do on our own, we've always got to lean into Him. He is the Creator of our souls and therefore the one who is able to make whole what is broken.

Fixing Our Gaze on Jesus

"Looking unto Jesus, the author and finisher of our faith, who for the joy that was set before Him endured the cross, despising the shame, and has sat down at the right hand of the throne of God" (Hebrews 12:2). This verse charges us to look unto Jesus! The question becomes, On what are you fixing your gaze? Where is your attention?

You see, your mind has eyes; that's how imagination works. You see the possibility of what could be with your mind's eye when you imagine it. You will always move in the direction of your sight. What are you dwelling on, and what imaginations are you empowering? Conversely, what imaginations are you disempowering by rebuking them? One way that your mind gets in trouble is when you depart from the bedrock of godly thinking. By godly thinking, I'm saying to plant your mind in God's way of doing things. You don't plant your mind in what culture dictates, but what the Bible promises you! You make war with the Word of God. To look at the Word is to look at Jesus.

It also says in this verse that Jesus is a finisher. There's a revelation of grace in this passage. You must learn to rely on the work of Jesus above your own flesh! Self-reliance will give way to a religious spirit, and that will steal your joy, your oil, and the flow of God in your life! God wants to empower you to break the slave mentality, in which you work and struggle continually but never get to your destination. When you rest in the finished work of Jesus, it empowers peace. You recognize that He has provided everything you need at Calvary, including your deliverance and emotional healing.

How do I effectively fix my gaze on Jesus? Here are specific ways:

- *Worship.* This is the exaltation of Jesus through personal worship and surrender. Worship is not limited to a church service. We need to worship Him daily.
- *Reading.* It is critical to be intentional about feeding your mind and spirit on the Word of God and godly teaching. The world is doing its best to disciple us and inundate us with its theories and philosophy. We must soak our minds in the Word of God.
- *Bible study.* This is digging deeper into the Bible! Do word studies, thematic studies, verse mapping—and if you don't know what some of these mean, go to Google ASAP! Become a student of the Word of God. It will feed you.
- *Meditation in the Word.* We have previously discussed this! It means to murmur, to ponder, and to digest with the mind.
- *Prophecy.* The prophetic builds up and testifies of Jesus. What has the Lord already declared over you? Stand on it. Decree it and fight the devil's lies with it.
- *Targeted prayer.* Aim the promise at the problem! Pray about it and aim your faith at it. Faith moves mountains.

Avoiding Emotional Shipwreck

What the devil wants to do is to keep you in a place I call "emotional shipwreck." Your faith feels faint, the promise seems distant, and you find yourself struggling again and again with the same problem and no solution. Let's look at some ways to avoid emotional shipwreck.

Refuse to waste time and thought on things you cannot change! The enemy loves to get you stuck in toxic thinking by tying you up in drama and futile emotional battles. You need to very quickly recognize that there are things you cannot change; give them to God in prayer. This is going to free your mind. I know from personal experience that I've often chosen to take on other people's problems. This may tie into our own childhoods and the false burdens that were put upon us. But part of our healing and deliverance is learning it's not our responsibility to carry these things! That one revelation will set you free.

Don't get stuck in the trap of people-pleasing! You are absolutely called to walk in love, but that does not mean being a person without healthy life patterns and relationships. This means you're going to have to say no at times. Healthy boundaries are going to help you remove yourself from situations, people, and places that are toxic. Don't apologize for your quest to stay and remain healthy. Don't allow your emotional and spiritual batteries to be zapped because you're overcommitting and saying yes to everything.

Forget about the past. I know this is much more easily said than done, but you cannot move forward while looking in the rearview mirror. You should absolutely learn from past seasons and rejoice in past victories, but do not live there. The enemy will try to keep your mind stuck in reverse to distract and disempower you from making forward progress. You may have to be very firm with yourself and very oppositional with the enemy. Quote the Word of God over your mind daily and refuse to go backward.

You need to take some faith risks! If you take no risk, you're going to have no reward. Emotionally strong people take calculated risks. Notice I said "calculated" because they're not foolish. When you are walking by faith, you're doing what God said. You're walking in obedience to Him. If it's a risk in your business, you've already done your research. If you're convinced it's the right direction for you, it's not dangerous or foolish. You've weighed the potential downsides, you've pondered what God said about it, and you can launch forward in an audacious move. Don't play it safe and later regret the fact that you did not step out.

Quit playing the comparison game and wishing you had somebody else's success! Your destiny is individual. It is not going to look like anybody else's. Your season and timing are different from that of the people around you. It's easy to judge someone from a faraway perspective, but you don't know the struggles and the battles they faced to get where they are. When you feel yourself becoming jealous or bitter concerning somebody else's promotion, stop right then. Pray for that person! This knocks the enemy off the throne of your heart and stops the comparison game. Instead, start to sow a seed of gratitude in your own heart for where you are and what God is doing in you and through you.

Don't put God on a time clock. Sometimes we struggle in our emotional health because we want immediate results. Everything God does begins with the release of a seed. It's in Genesis 8:22 that while the earth remains, there'll be seedtime and harvest. This means there'll be a season of sacrifice, a season of waiting, and then the harvest comes. Sometimes we are frustrated because we're stuck in the part of the process called "the wait." But we learn the greatest lessons when we're waiting upon the Lord. We experience levels and realms of His presence when we're waiting upon the Lord that we'll never experience otherwise. We encounter people critical to our destiny as we wait upon the Lord. Learn to be thankful for the wait— you will eventually come into the harvest!

A Journey of Heart Healing

"Trust in the LORD with all your heart, and lean not on your own understanding; in all your ways acknowledge Him, and He shall direct your paths" (Proverbs 3:5–6). Embarking on a journey of heart healing means first returning to the lordship of Jesus. It's the recognition that He is in charge, not us. We recognize that we can rest in the sovereignty of God, and trust Him with every step on our path. This means thanking God in the unknown spaces. All too often, we become control freaks! We want to dictate the when, the how, and the why. The reality is, when we yielded our lives to Jesus, we gave Him control over those areas.

"Now faith is the substance of things hoped for, the evidence of things not seen" (Hebrews 11:1). Healing is a journey of faith. We must understand that faith is a substance, not a concept or idea. I remember years ago my spiritual father said to me, "You can't believe God just because you want to."

At the time, I didn't really understand what he meant, and I was intrigued by this statement. Why can't a person just believe God because they want to? As I reflected on his statement, the answer became clear to me. Faith is the byproduct of hearing from God, according to Romans 10:17. When God speaks, faith is released! Therefore, I am unable to simply make a mental decision to walk by faith about my healing, my finances, or my sanctification. Faith comes when I first hear from God regarding those areas. So if I'm dealing with my emotional health, I need to get faith in the realm of emotional healing. It is a substance, which means I can lean on it and rely upon it. Just as a table is a substance that my hands can touch, so is faith a spiritual substance that my spirit and my life can touch. It is a spiritual substance that will uphold me in times of instability and crisis.

Faith is not bound to a time clock. Too many believers try to dictate to God when He needs to come through for them. But to really walk out your healing journey, you've got to yield to the process. It is a daily choice to believe God, no matter what you're feeling or what you're seeing with your natural eyes. It is a daily choice to cling to the Word of God and put it above the circumstance and affairs of life. I want to encourage you as you are in your process of healing not to quit or give up. One thing is for certain: If you quit, you're never going to make it to the other side. But if you hold on, you will perhaps break through and become the bloodline breaker God has called you to be.

"I will bless the Lord at all times; His praise shall continually be in my mouth" (Psalm 34:1). "All times" does not mean sometimes! When we praise God only when we feel emotional, we limit the operation of God's power in our lives. To embrace the heart-healing, emotion-healing journey we are on, we've got to learn to praise God in everything. This means we choose to lift up His promises above the issues. We choose to give God praise at *all times*, including adverse times—so we are telling our minds and our bodies to submit to the reality of God. We are stating that God's promises trump our current circumstances. Praise is a prophetic prediction. When I praise God, I am prophesying over my future. What would it look like if you radically praised God during an attack? In the spirit realm, you would be solidifying the solution by establishing Him as Lord over your crisis and your feelings!

"And He said to me, 'My grace is sufficient for you, for My strength is made perfect in weakness.' Therefore most gladly I will rather boast in my infirmities, that the power of Christ may rest upon me" (2 Corinthians 12:9). Grace is a necessary ingredient for soul healing. We sometimes think we should hide our insufficiencies from God, but He already knows them. We should bring our pain and struggle before the Lord and let Him pour His grace into it. He knew that you would have these struggles before they ever began! He knew that you would be battling some of the things you're battling today before you ever entered human existence. He has loved you despite every insufficiency and shortcoming! His grace is an operation of His love, and when we bring our weakness before Him, His strength is poured into it! God does not need your talent or skill; He simply needs your yes.

Grace is walking with God in great confidence that He loves you regardless of your actions. Grace is finding beauty even in your missteps. Grace is the ability to recognize that your salvation had very little to do with you, and everything to do with the finished work of Jesus upon the cross. When grace becomes a part of your healing process, you don't give up when you stumble. You realize that even the stumbling draws you closer to the Lord. You begin to see His footprints and His hand at work in every season of your life, including the darkest ones. When you fully embrace the grace of God, you will also begin to have grace toward yourself! This is perhaps one of the most vital ingredients of your total healing journey. You're going to find that at times, you fall back down. You're going to experience moments in which you do the thing you know you should not do. Paul had those moments. It was in keeping in step with the Spirit that Paul had the freedom he so greatly desired. Intrinsic to that walk is the manifestation of the grace of God. Let grace do its work in your life today!

"It shall come to pass in that day that his burden will be taken away from your shoulder, and his yoke from your neck, and the yoke will be destroyed because of the anointing oil" (Isaiah 10:27). Tap into the anointing of God on your healing journey. God's anointing is His *super* upon your *natural*! It is the power of God to do the thing you are called to do. You see, God provided not just the purpose but also the power. The anointing destroys yokes and bondages off your life. When you rest under the flow of His anointing, you rest under the flow of deliverance. You rest under the flow of healing and recovery and under the flow of victory and abundance. Make much of the anointing and the anointing will make much of you! Listen to anointed worship songs and praise God during them! Invite anointed people to lay hands on you and pray and prophesy over your life. Get into anointed environments and atmospheres. Host the anointing in your home by welcoming the Holy Spirit and inviting His presence into your four walls! Be sensitive to the moving of His Spirit; this will catapult you forward into your journey of recovery!

"If we live in the Spirit, let us also walk in the Spirit" (Galatians 5:25). Walk it out! Your healing journey requires daily steps. We can become overwhelmed by looking at the size of a struggle. But remember, the size of our struggle is small in comparison to the size of our God! Second, remember that greatness happens in small steps and seeds. We must continue to be committed to move forward daily in God. Some days, that may mean only one step forward. Other days, perhaps it's fifteen steps forward. The important thing is we stay in motion on a daily, consistent basis! Jesus has a wonderful journey He wants to take you on! He wants to plant your soul in green pastures, where still waters shimmer. This means a place of peace, abundance, purpose, and power! You are at your best when you are walking in alignment with His will for you.

Learning to Walk in Emotional Health

Ask yourself these questions in response to what we've discussed in this chapter about healing emotionally: *Have I realized the role Jesus plays as the Good Shepherd in my life? Do I understand how profound His grace toward me is? Am I taking daily steps in my journey? Am I okay with being vulnerable in His presence and calling on Him for help?*

These are all points of evaluation as you receive Jesus' healing power in your life. He takes delight in your wholeness as a child of God. He wants your mind to be healthy so that your life is healthy.

Give yourself grace as you journey through the wild emotions that you will encounter in your heart-healing journey. When we learn how to walk in health in our emotions, we slam the door shut to emotional manipulation and the lies the enemy tells.

LET'S REFLECT

1. Healing demands intentional pursuit. What are some ways you can pursue emotional healing?
2. What do you tend to fix your gaze upon the most? What claims your attention? How can you practically pursue setting your gaze on Jesus more consistently?
3. List a time when you experienced emotional shipwreck. What can you do to avoid arriving at that place again?
4. Choose and write out a scripture you will cling to through your healing process. Commit this scripture to memory, so that you can repeat it anytime you need it.

CHAPTER TEN

Decrees and Prayers

Now that we have begun a journey of freedom, I want to equip you with tools to fight the enemy and solidify your breakthrough. As Spirit-filled believers, we have been granted the authority and power to decree and activate God's power in our lives. The Word of God declares, "You will also declare a thing, and it will be established for you; so light will shine on your ways" (Job 22:28). Through our decrees, we align ourselves with the will of God and release His wonder-working power in our lives. Along with decreeing, we can approach the throne of grace with prayer and petition, asking God for supernatural transformation in every area of our lives. The Bible teaches us the value of prayer, declaring, "Be anxious for nothing, but in everything by prayer and supplication, with thanksgiving, let your requests be made known to God" (Philippians 4:6). Decrees and prayers will help you stand against the enemy and secure your victory!

Decree over My Steps

Thank you, Lord, that you've ordained the path for me.
Thank you, Lord, that you are revealing the path to me without hindrance or delay.
Thank you, Lord, that you are sending destiny partners to assist me to navigate my path.
Thank you, Lord, that you're upholding my feet when the enemy comes with adversity.
Thank you, Lord, that you are sustaining me on my journey.
I decree that my steps are ordered of heaven!
I decree that I walk with you daily.
I decree that I am led by your Spirit in my daily steps.
I hear your voice, I do your will, and I obey your instructions.
I decree that my steps are ordered, my path is secure, and my way is clear, in Jesus' name, Amen.

The steps of a good man are ordered by the LORD: and he delights in his way.

Psalm 37:23

Decree to Break Rejection

I decree that I'm accepted in the Beloved.
I decree that the love of God dwells in me and brings continual freedom to my life.
I decree that rejection cannot manifest itself through me, in Jesus' name!

I decree that every demon of rejection has to leave me, in the name of Jesus.

I decree that rejected thinking must bow to the Word of God.

I decree that my mind dwells in the peace of God and His acceptance.

I decree that every orphan spirit must go from me, in Jesus' name.

I decree that I am a child of God and no longer an orphan.

I decree that because I'm free from rejection, I do not manifest rejection in my relationships with others.

I decree that I have mature and godly relationships.

I decree that I have a healthy view of others.

I decree that I'm loving toward others and walk in the love of God.

I decree that because I have a revelation of God's grace in my life, I am graceful toward others.

I break and bind every spirit of rejection and command it to go from me now, in Jesus' name, Amen!

"I will be a Father to you, and you shall be My sons and daughters," says the Lord Almighty.

2 Corinthians 6:18

Decree for Guidance

I decree, Lord, that I am led by your Holy Spirit.

I decree that I clearly hear your voice.

I decree that I'm not deceived, in Jesus' name.

I decree that I'm sensitive to your leading and guidance.

I decree that because I'm your child, hearing is my portion.

I clearly hear and know your voice!

I am not deceived by the voice of a stranger.

I will not disobey the directions of my Father!

I am your child, I receive your instructions, and I follow your leading in every facet of my life, in Jesus' name, Amen.

For as many as are led by the Spirit of God, these are sons of God.

Romans 8:14

Decree for the Mind of Christ

I decree that I have the mind of Christ, in Jesus' name!

I decree that I think like Christ.

I decree that thoughts of confusion must leave me, in Jesus' name.

I decree that deceiving thoughts must go from me, in Jesus' name.

I decree that the lies of the enemy over my mind are broken, in Jesus' name.

I decree that my mind operates in the peace of God.

I decree that I think God-centered thoughts.

I decree that I dream audacious God-dreams.

I decree that fear has no place in my thought life.

I decree that I walk in the wisdom of God and think wise thoughts.

I decree that because I think wise thoughts, I speak wise words.

I decree that I am a person of wisdom.

I decree that the wisdom of God is my portion and the peace of God is my reality.

I decree that I hear from God and I embrace His way of thinking.

I decree that my mind belongs to God, in the name of Jesus!

I decree that my mind is sanctified and separated for the purposes and plans of God.

I take authority over every lying spirit that would try to attack my mind, in the name of Jesus!

I take authority over the spirit of fear and forbid its operation in my thought life, in Jesus' name.

I take authority over false accusations that would try to harass my mind, in Jesus' name.

I thank you, Lord, that I meditate and dwell upon the truth of your Word and that your promises are for me, in the name of Jesus.

Thank you, Lord, that I have access to your way of thinking, your way of living, in the reality of my new nature.

I decree that your mind is in me and working through my thought life, in the name of Jesus, Amen.

Let this mind be in you which was also in Christ Jesus.

Philippians 2:5

Decree for Right Connections

I decree glorious and divine connections in my life.

God, you are sending the right people to my life, in the name of Jesus.

God, you are removing the wrong people from my life, in Jesus' name.

I decree destiny partners in my life.

I decree right relationships in my life.

I decree that I am not deceived in my relationships, but I embrace the right people for the right purpose.

I decree that I am supernaturally led, and will be connected to the people whom God has ordained for me.

I decree that my relationships are sanctified, in the name of Jesus.

I decree that God leads me in my relationships and I connect with God-ordained people.

I decree the right relationships at the right time, in the name of Jesus, Amen.

As iron sharpens iron, so a man sharpens the countenance of his friend.

Proverbs 27:17

Decree for Wisdom

I decree that I walk in wisdom.

I seek the Lord, and therefore wisdom is my portion.

I decree that uncommon wisdom is upon me and manifesting in every area of my life.

I am a person who walks in supernatural and uncommon wisdom.

Wisdom unlocks the favor of God, and favor makes room for me.

Favor brings the right people into my life, and brings me into the right spaces.

I decree that I make wise decisions.

I decree that I walk with wise people.

I decree that I move in wisdom concerning the timing of God in my life.

I walk in unusual levels of prosperity, because uncommon wisdom brings favor and success in my life.

I pray wise prayers.

I speak wise words.

I have wise friends.

Thank you, Lord, for supernatural and unusual wisdom in my life, in Jesus' name, Amen.

For the LORD gives wisdom; from His mouth come knowledge and understanding.

Proverbs 2:6

Decree Against Emotional Witchcraft

I command every demon of witchcraft to be broken over my life, in the name of Jesus!

I command demons of manipulation and control to leave me, in Jesus' name!

I break the power of every lying and deceptive demon that would try to influence my life, in the name of Jesus.

Thank you, Lord, that my discernment is razor-sharp, in Jesus' name.

I decree that I discern wrong relationships and motives.

I decree that I see and sense hidden demonic operations.

I decree that I will not be bound or controlled by the will of another person; I am controlled by the will of God.

I decree that all operations of manipulation and control against me are revealed and exposed, in the name of Jesus.

I decree that I am free from every manipulating power and spirit, in the name of Jesus, Amen.

Decree for Spiritual Senses

I decree that I am quick to pay attention to your voice, Lord, in dreams and visions.

I decree that I stop and focus in on what you want to show me.

I decree that my spiritual ears are open to hear your voice.

I clearly hear you speaking and discern your leading in my life.

I am effectively led by your Spirit and move when you say to move.

I decree bold obedience and clarity.

Thank you, Lord, for speaking to me in the night season.

Thank you, Lord, for prophetic visions and dreams.

I host your voice!

I discern your voice.

I honor your voice.

I heed your voice, in the name of Jesus, Amen.

Decree for Victory

I decree that the Lord is fighting my battles.

I rest in the Lord, and in the power of His might, to protect and preserve me!

I don't yield to fear or anxiety.

I walk in abundant, supernatural peace.

God has never lost the battle, and therefore I rest in His supreme victory over my life.

God is fighting for me in every area of my life, from my relationships to my finances.

I decree that because I trust the Lord, I am not disappointed.

I decree that He is guiding my steps and securing them with His power.

I decree that I walk in a spirit of discernment concerning my relationships.

I decree that when the enemy tries to sabotage my relationships, God brings divine protection and preservation.

I decree that the Lord is my champion, and His protection is abundant in my life, in Jesus' name.

I decree that no weapon formed against me shall prosper!

I decree that no lie will stand against me.

I bind and break lying spirits over my life, in Jesus' name.

I bind and break lies that are trying to come against my mind.

I bind and break lying reports.

I refuse to think lying thoughts.

I refuse to accept lies connected to my past.

The Lord has delivered me from my past, and I'm walking in newness by the blood of Jesus.

I can rest in the knowledge that the battle has already been won and the victory is secured for me, in Jesus' name.

I will enjoy the spoils of my enemy because the Lord has brought me the victory, in Jesus' name, Amen.

The Lord will fight for you.

Exodus 14:14

Prayer for Healing a Broken Heart

Thank you, Lord, that you came to heal the brokenhearted! I lift every wound and pain in my heart to you. You are my healer and deliverer. Your blood has made me free. I call upon your healing power right now. I invite you into my heart to heal and deliver me from all pain in my emotions. I believe that your healing power is working in my life right now. I bind and break all brokenness. I receive your healing power in my mind and emotions now, in the name of Jesus, Amen.

Peace I leave with you, My peace I give to you; not as the world gives do I give to you. Do not let your heart be troubled, nor let it be fearful.

John 14:27

Prayer to Break Free from Condemnation

Thank you, Lord, for your healing power in my life. I receive my inheritance and full adoption, and as a child of God, I am accepted and not condemned. I will not partner with a lying and condemning spirit. My Bible says that I am accepted in the Beloved. I say to my mind, "You are accepted, so quit entertaining rejection and condemnation." I cast those thoughts down. I break condemnation and command it to go from me, in Jesus' name, Amen.

There is therefore now no condemnation for those who are in Christ Jesus.

Romans 8:1

Prayer to Break Confusion

I decree that I have a sound mind! I walk in the wisdom of God. I am led and directed by the Holy Spirit. I clearly hear, know, and see. I discern the will of God. I am not confused. I break the spirit of confusion over my life, in Jesus' name! I command every spirit of confusion to leave me, in the name of Jesus, Amen.

For God is not the author of confusion but of peace, as in all the churches of the saints.

1 Corinthians 14:33

Prayer to Break Controlling Demons

I decree that I am led by the Spirit of God. I am not dominated or controlled by any demon or person. I do not operate in manipulation or control toward others. I am not insecure. I do not exert unhealthy levels of domination over others. I am free from all controlling and manipulating spirits. My mind is free from thoughts of control. I am strong and not weak, in Jesus' name. I command all controlling spirits to go from me now, in Jesus' name! I break the power of manipulation off my life, in Jesus' name. Every stronghold of domination, be broken right now. I am free, in Jesus' name. Amen.

For as many as are led by the Spirit of God, these are sons of God. For you did not receive the spirit of bondage again to fear, but you received the Spirit of adoption by whom we cry out, "Abba, Father."

Romans 8:14–15

Prayer to Break the Spirit of Fear

God has not given me a spirit of fear. He has given me a spirit of power, love, and a sound mind. I cast out the spirit of fear and every type of fear, in Jesus' name. I command fear to flee from my life now. Spirit of fear, go right now, in Jesus' name! I say that I am free of all fear.

For God has not given us a spirit of fear, but of power and of love and of a sound mind.

2 Timothy 1:7

Prayer to Recover from Hurt

Lord, I thank you that you are my healer. I invite your healing power into every part of my life right now. I open my heart and mind before you, Lord, and I thank you that you said you came to heal the brokenhearted. I release every hurt and wound to you, Lord. I command the power of hurt to be broken off my life, in Jesus' name. I break your power and command you to go from me, in Jesus' name. I refuse to be stuck in a cycle of hurt and wounds. Jesus, you set me free! I believe that I am free indeed.

The righteous cry out, and the LORD hears, and delivers them out of all their troubles. The LORD is near to those who have a broken heart, and saves such as have a contrite spirit.

Psalm 34:17–18

Prayer for Soul Healing

Lord, I thank you that you are my Good Shepherd and you lead me beside still waters. You restore my soul, my mind, my will, and my emotions. I thank you, Lord, that you are healing every broken place of my emotional heart. I open my heart before you, Lord, and I ask you to examine every portion of it. Lord, I'm asking for your healing power to be poured into my heart. I acknowledge that you alone direct my paths and restore my soul. I thank you, Lord, that you said in Luke 4:18 that you came to heal the brokenhearted, and I expect your healing power to move in every area of my life. I thank you, Lord, that you bring me to green pastures, places of prosperity and abundance. I thank you, Lord, that you bring me to places of healing and recovery, in the name of Jesus. Lord, today I'm inviting you into my heart, into my mind, and into my memories to heal every part, in Jesus' name, Amen.

The Lord is my shepherd; I shall not want. He makes me to lie down in green pastures; He leads me beside the still waters. He restores my soul;
He leads me in the paths of righteousness for His name's sake.

Psalm 23:1–3

Prayer over Friendships

Father, I come before you now with a heart full of gratitude for the gift of friendship. I decree and declare that my life is surrounded by right friends, in Jesus' name! Thank you for those who are aligned with your purpose and destiny for my life. Thank you for giving me discernment and wisdom to steward these relationships well, in the name of Jesus, Amen.

A man who has friends must himself be friendly, but there is a friend who sticks closer than a brother.

Proverbs 18:24

I decree that I am friendly and show myself friendly, attracting friends who are closer than a brother, loyal, and trustworthy.

As iron sharpens iron, so a man sharpens the countenance of his friend.

Proverbs 27:17

I declare that my friends sharpen me, and I sharpen them. We challenge and encourage each other to grow in wisdom and godliness.

Do not be deceived: "Evil company corrupts good habits."

1 Corinthians 15:33

I decree that my circle of friends consists of those who uphold good morals and godly character, and I distance myself from any corrupt influences.

Two are better than one, because they have a good reward for their labor. For if they fall, one will lift up his companion.

But woe to him who is alone when he falls, for he has no one to help him up.

Ecclesiastes 4:9–10

I declare that I have friends who lift me up when I fall, and I do the same for them. Together, we achieve great things and support each other in times of need.

A friend loves at all times, and a brother is born for adversity.

Proverbs 17:17

I decree that my friends love at all times, and we stand by each other through adversity, reflecting the love and support that Christ has for us.

Lord, I thank you for aligning me with the right people. I thank you for faith friends who push me higher in the realm of the Spirit. I thank you that I pour into my friendships with grace and love. I thank you that I am a faithful friend and that I have godly friends in my life, in the name of Jesus, Amen.

Prayer over Marriage

Lord, I come before you in the name of Jesus, lifting my marriage to you. I thank you that marriage is a sacred covenant you designed, and I praise you for the blessing of my spouse. I ask for your divine protection over our union, and I stand against any forces of darkness that seek to harm us, sow seeds of strife, or divide us in any way.

For we do not wrestle against flesh and blood, but against principalities, against powers, against the rulers of the darkness of this age, against spiritual hosts of wickedness in the heavenly places.

Ephesians 6:12

I know that battles we face in our marriage are not just physical but spiritual, and I decree that I see and discern unseen opponents. I take authority over every demon that seeks to attack our relationship. In the name of Jesus, I bind and cast out any spirit of division, misunderstanding, or strife that tries to enter our marriage and create division. I command you to go, in the name of Jesus!

Though one may be overpowered by another, two can withstand him. And a threefold cord is not quickly broken.

Ecclesiastes 4:12

I declare that my spouse and I walk in unity in the name of Jesus. We stand together against any adversary, and we stand with you, Lord, to form a threefold cord that is not easily broken. I invite you, Holy Spirit, to be the center of our marriage, binding us together in perfect love, unity, and agreement. I recognize that there is great power in agreement, and I decree that we walk in agreement, in the name of Jesus.

Lord, I thank you for understanding, patience, wisdom, and grace between my spouse and me. Help our relationship to be wise and void of strife. Help us to walk in your love and forgiveness one toward the other so that we may do your will.

I decree that no demonic weapon formed against our marriage shall prosper, according to Isaiah 54:17. I thank you, Lord, that we are covered by the blood of Jesus, and that our home is a place of peace, love, and joy. Strengthen our bond and help us grow deeper in love with each other daily. Help us put you first and to grow in our love and passion for you, Lord. In the mighty name of Jesus I pray, Amen.

Prayer over All Relationships

I thank you, Lord, that I walk in maturity in all my relationships, in the name of Jesus.

I thank you, Lord, that I honor spiritual leaders and those whom you've sent to impart into my life.

I thank you, Lord, that I respect and give reverence to the relationships that you've brought into my life.

I thank you, Lord, that I am growing in maturity, in grace, in favor, and in wisdom.

I thank you, Lord, that I understand the value of kingdom relationships and I prioritize them as you lead me.

I thank you, Lord, that I'm a person of great wisdom and strength.

I thank you, Lord, that I do not embrace toxic or manipulative relationships, but I shun them and draw the appropriate boundaries.

Give me wisdom, Lord, to know which relationships to prioritize.

Give me strength to say no when I need to say no.

Give me faith to believe in your audacious dreams for my life.

Give me discernment to know and welcome the destiny partners whom you are sending to me. I give each and every relationship in my life to you, Lord, and I ask you to make me a good steward of those relationships, in Jesus' name, Amen.

Acknowledgments

Thank you to my wife, my boo, my forever love—Joy LeStrange. We have been together on this wild journey called life for half of our lives! You are like fine wine; you get better with age.

Thank you to my mom, Eileen Hromin, for always believing in me and pushing me forward.

Thank you to my son, Josh, and stepfather, Zeljko. I love you both. You are amazing men.

Thank you to all of my family. You are loved, known, and seen.

Thank you to my late spiritual father, Dr. Norvel Hayes—you saw me, imparted to me, trained me, and pushed me.

Thank you to my apostolic leader, Apostle John Eckhardt. You are a brilliant pioneer who keeps bringing the next generation forth with great love and wisdom.

Thank you to my friends and partners.

Thank you to my mentees and students.

Thank you to my staff for the support and dedication.

Acknowledgments

Thank you to Global Hub and ATL Hub members and team. We are shaking nations together.

I have nothing but love for each of you! You have all been a tremendous part of my journey.

Notes

Chapter 2 The Nice Church Lady
1. Bible Study Tools, "exousia" (Strong's #1849), accessed March 17, 2025, https://www.biblestudytools.com/lexicons/greek/kjv/exousia.html.
2. Bible Study Tools, "epiginosko" (Strong's #1921), accessed March 17, 2025, https://www.biblestudytools.com/lexicons/greek/kjv/epiginosko.html.

Chapter 3 The Purpose of Godly Relationships
1. *Merriam-Webster Dictionary*, "favor," accessed March 17, 2025, https://www.merriam-webster.com/dictionary/favor.

Chapter 5 Types of Manipulators
1. Bible Study Tools, "leb" (Strong's #3820), accessed March 18, 2025, https://www.biblestudytools.com/lexicons/hebrew/kjv/leb.html.

Chapter 6 Closing Open Doorways
1. *Merriam-Webster Dictionary*, "discernment," accessed March 18, 2025, https://www.merriam-webster.com/dictionary/discernment.

Chapter 7 Breaking Soul Ties and Evil Alliances
1. *Merriam-Webster Dictionary*, "renounce," accessed March 19, 2025, https://www.merriam-webster.com/dictionary/renounce.

Ryan LeStrange is a dynamic apostolic and prophetic leader with a passion for global awakening. He is the founder of Global Hub, a global online church, and ATL Hub Church, having its in-person expression in Atlanta. He also leads the Hub Apostolic Network, a global network of ministers, governing churches, and Apostolic Hubs.

Beyond ministry, Ryan is a visionary entrepreneur and a pioneer in digital media, committed to equipping believers through cutting-edge content, e-courses, mentorship, and prophetic resources. He leads LeStrange Global LLC, a faith-based media company dedicated to empowering a new generation of leaders.

He is the author of numerous books, including *Supernatural Access* and *Overcoming Spiritual Attacks*. Ryan and his wife, Joy, reside in the Atlanta area, where they continue to impact lives through ministry, media, and leadership development.

Connect with Ryan

RyanLeStrange.com

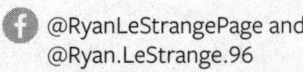 @RyanLeStrangePage and @Ryan.LeStrange.96

 @RyanLeStrange